SWAN LAKE

SADLER'S WELLS ROYAL BALLET
SWAN LAKE

Barbara Newman & Leslie E. Spatt

DANCE BOOKS
9 Cecil Court London WC2

First published in 1983
by Dance Books Ltd.,
9 Cecil Court, London WC2N 4EZ.

ISBN 0 903102 72 2

Designed by Jim Reader
Design and production in association
with Book Production Consultants.
47 Norfolk Street, Cambridge CB1 2LE

Typeset by Glyn Davies Typesetting

Printed in Great Britain by William Clowes (Beccles) Limited,
Beccles and London

Bound by The Garden City Press Limited, Herts.

INTRODUCTION

In the last paragraph of the Royal Opera House press release of 10 February, 1981, with absolutely no fanfare whatever, the Sadler's Wells Royal Ballet announced a new production of *Swan Lake* for its autumn season. Peter Wright, the company's director, and Galina Samsova, one of its ballerinas and teachers, would share the task of staging the ballet. They would also rechoreograph those sections of it which have long ceased to be the work of Lev Ivanov and Marius Petipa, its original choreographers. Philip Prowse would design the settings and costumes; Barry Wordsworth, the company's principal conductor, would take charge of the orchestra and Tchaikovsky's great score.

The majority of this press release was devoted to plans for the Royal Ballet's fiftieth anniversary celebrations. Neither it nor, as it happened, any other release ever outlined the balance of the Sadler's Wells Royal Ballet's autumn schedule, which included three weeks in the Big Top in Plymouth, a whirlwind two-week tour of Yugoslavia, and a two-week residency in London on its home stage at the Sadler's Wells Theatre.

If you skim through a schedule like that, you'll probably register only the proper names: *Swan Lake*, Big Top, Yugoslavia. But if you read it over again, more slowly, three tiny words will suddenly overshadow all the other dates and details. "A new production" is easily said and quickly read, but its implications are boundless.

Mounting a new production of *Swan Lake*, or of any great classical ballet, cannot be compared to any other theatrical venture of any kind. It is wholly unlike restaging an opera or a play, for very simple reasons. If you announce a new production of *Tosca,* you might have new ideas about the action or the characters' motivations, but the audience will still expect to hear *Tosca* exactly as Puccini wrote it. Every note sung, every part in the orchestra, is written down, fixed, and cannot be changed. But in *Swan Lake*, virtually nothing is fixed. The original title, *Le Lac des Cygnes*, is never used any more, and much of the original choreography is lost. The story and characters remain largely unchanged in every production, but most of the actual steps are new. So are the designs and the arrangement of the music, which has been rewritten and reorganized—only sometimes by Tchaikovsky—innumerable times.

The last time the company now known as the Sadler's Wells Royal Ballet performed *Swan Lake* was in 1970, when most of the dancers in the present company were between eight and fifteen years old. Today, some of them have still never seen the ballet, much less appeared in it. So, before this proposed production can exist, someone with more experience will have to teach them a style of dancing which is new to them as well as approximately three hours of new steps. Even the remaining bits of the original work, like the famous dance of the cygnets, are completely new if you've never danced them or even seen them. And since the company numbers only fifty, many dancers will have to appear in more than one role in the course of a single performance. How will they ever learn the ballet? How long will it take? Who will teach them?

And once Philip Prowse has decided how he wants his swans to look, as opposed to any other flock of swans that ever danced beside a painted lake, he will translate his ideas for their costumes into drawings and someone else will translate his drawings into reality. Someone will have to buy the fabrics he has chosen, cut them, sew them, decorate them. Who will do all this work? Where will the fabrics come from? When will they be assembled?

Philip Prowse will also design a lakeside scene, and a ballroom, and thrones, lanterns and crossbows, props that no self-respecting *Swan Lake* would be without. How will these designs travel from his imagination to the stage?

Announcing a new production is rather like announcing a small invasion. Thousands of decisions have to be made, variables discarded, questions asked and answered, before the work can be launched before an audience. New productions of ballets don't emerge from cardboard boxes on opening night, and nothing stops while they are conceived, designed, rehearsed and constructed. While Peter Wright's *Swan Lake* was in preparation, I asked the people preparing it about their work. Here are some of their answers, for which I offer this book in thanks. It is dedicated to them, to their skill, their art, and their own unflagging dedication.

B.N.

London

October 1982

8 September. Twelve weeks to opening night. On the first day of the autumn season in the Sadler's Wells Theatre, *Swan Lake* is nowhere to be seen. Every corner of the theatre is crammed and busy—stage, orchestra pit, studios, wardrobe. There is too much to prepare for the company's two-week season, too many ballets to rehearse, too many injured dancers to replace, for anyone to waste a moment on a work that won't face an audience for another three months. The immediate present has first claim on everyone's attention, and it demands twelve to fifteen hours a day from the dancers and staff.

But don't think the work on *Lac* hasn't begun; it has only been suspended temporarily. Peter Wright started choreographing months ago, before the company's June season at the Royal Opera House. "I got the go-ahead the beginning of '81," he told me, "and I started with all the new stuff, the Act 1 waltz, the Polacca, so I'd have time to change them. I was nervous—most choreographers are in the first few days, until you find your way, especially when you're touching something that's sacred in a way. It's only when you see new things in context, as part of the whole, that you know if they'll succeed."

But those early rehearsals are already history. *Les Sylphides* and *Night Moves* need rehearsing today, and *La Fille mal gardée* and *Checkmate*, and the audience arrives every night. The only tangible proof that *Swan Lake* exists at all is pinned to the dancers' callboard outside the rehearsal studio. Down in one corner below the current rehearsal schedules, there are three pages of provisional casting for *Swan Lake*, and a three page synopsis of the ballet as well, both dated August '81. They are grimy with handling, as if the dancers have been reading them, over and over, since the day they were posted. They scan the casting—any casting—with apparent casualness, but their own names leap off the page at them like banners, proclaiming the relative success of their efforts to be noticed and singled out. As to the fingerprints on the synopsis . . . well, even the story of *Swan Lake* can be new if you're only eighteen. This is the way Peter Wright has told it:

Act I: A Courtyard in the Castle
Following his father's death, Prince Siegfried will shortly be crowned King and must therefore marry. He dreads the loss of his freedom and has no wish to choose a bride he does not love. It is the night of his 21st birthday and his friends at court have assembled to present him with the gift of a cross-bow. His equerry and friend, Benno, has arranged an entertainment to divert him but in the midst of these celebrations the Queen Mother arrives, unannounced. She is shocked at the revelry while the court is still officially in mourning and reminds Siegfried that the following day he must choose a

bride. She departs leaving Siegfried despondent. Benno attempts to cheer him with the help of two girls and the men then join in a drinking dance to toast the future King. When the dancers have gone, a flight of swans passes and Benno suggests that Siegfried try out his new cross-bow. They depart in pursuit.

Act II: The Lakeside by Moonlight

On arrival at the lakeside Prince Siegfried sends Benno in search of the swans. Left alone he becomes aware of an evil presence—the magician, Baron von Rothbart. Suddenly a swan approaches and Siegfried watches in amazement as it is transformed into a beautiful maiden. She is the Princess Odette. She and her companions have been turned into swans by Baron von Rothbart and only at night can they return to human form. Odette's enchantment can be broken only if someone who has never loved before swears an oath of undying love to her. He declares his love and swears to be true for eternity. When von Rothbart appears Prince Siegfried attempts to shoot him, but Odette intercedes explaining that if the magician dies the spell can never be broken. She warns him that if he breaks his vow of love she must remain a swan forever. Dawn approaches and she and her companions return to the lake and resume their guise as swans.

Act III: The Ballroom of the Castle

At a grand reception Prince Siegfried must choose his bride from three princesses. They each dance for him but his thoughts are elsewhere and he refuses to make a choice. A fanfare announces the arrival of two uninvited guests; they are von Rothbart, disguised as an Ambassador, and his daughter Odile, whom the Sorcerer has transformed to look like Odette. The Prince is taken in by the unknown visitor's startling resemblance to Odette and believes her to be the Swan Princess. While Odile and the Prince dance together a vision of Odette appears beseeching Siegfried to remember his vow, but his attention is distracted by the magician's spell. Infatuated, Siegfried asks for Odile's hand in marriage. Von Rothbart makes him swear his love for her and as Siegfried does so, Odette appears at the window. It is too late; he has pledged his word to another. The court is thrown into confusion and in despair the Prince rushes out in search of his love.

Act IV: The Lakeside

Odette returns distraught to the swan-maidens, wishing to drown herself in the waters of the lake while she is still in human form. Realising Siegfried is following her, von Rothbart creates a storm in a vain attempt to stop him. Siegfried arrives and begs Odette's forgiveness. Sadly, she tells him that she forgives him but nothing can change the fact that his vow was broken. Odette and Siegfried decide they cannot live apart and will die together, thus breaking the spell. Odette throws herself into the lake and von Rothbart is thwarted in his attempt to stop Siegfried following her. As dawn breaks, the lovers are united in a world of eternal love.

Black Swan *pas de deux*. Galina Samsova and David Ashmole

Every morning until the end of the London season, Mme. Soulamif Messerer will teach a company class. Short and plump, with flyaway dark hair and darting dark eyes, she was a highly respected teacher in Russia after her retirement from the stage. This is her first position with a British company since her defection in 1980. "I am very happy to work with this company and very pleased with them all. Now I work more on the arms and *épaulement*. They all need that."

The difference between what the dancers already know and what Mme. Messerer—and Galina Samsova—can teach them is a difference of style. Russian dancers are justly famed for the subtle grace and fluidity of their arms and upper bodies, and for the way their movements seem to originate deep in the spine and flow outward through the limbs. Their dancing is embellished, and their carriage is aristocratic. And *Swan Lake* is a ballet that must be danced by proud, noble aristocrats with a tradition of privilege behind them. The work was, after all, created for the Tsar's Imperial Ballet.

As a guest teacher, Mme. Messerer has only a few weeks to impart this noble style to the company, but they are learning it anyway by watching Galina, who carries it in her bones. Her career began in Kiev, to which she has recently returned to study the production of *Swan Lake* she danced there, and the imprint of her training lies in every yielding curve and artful flourish of her dancing. The company made its first stab at the grand Russian style in her production of

9

Paquita in 1980, and the style will develop in them as they need it. They will learn to be Imperial by being Imperial. It is slow going.

Think of it this way: Imagine yourself in court dress of the nineteenth century. Could you convince someone–through your manner, your bearing, the pace and grace of your movements–that you lived inside those clothes, inside that leisured, protected society? Dancers must do this in every ballet: convince several hundred or thousand strangers that they are who they are pretending to be. The convincing starts in the studio and in class.

Mme. Messerer scolds one of them: "You don't believe *yourself*. You must *believe* yourself," and then adds quietly, "I danced for twenty-five years as prima ballerina at the Bolshoi. I know everything." She is teaching them how to dance *Swan Lake* even if she doesn't mean to, even if they don't know it.

Class is small. The girls wear red, cranberry, six different purples to brighten the grey morning. One of them has safety-pinned one ribbon neatly to her shoe, placing the pin exactly parallel to the floor. They all look tired and slightly pale when they wander into the Cranko Room atop the theatre, and tired but slightly flushed after class. As they leave, principal dancer and *répétiteur* Alain Dubreuil interrupts the general rush to the door. "Anyone involved in *Night Moves*, don't go away. Kim's off and Grahame's going to have to do it, so there'll be an emergency call." Translated from their standard shorthand, this means that Kim Reeder is injured and Grahame Lustig will have to replace him in David Bintley's ballet, rehearsing the role with its fiendishly difficult solo this afternoon and performing it for the first time this evening. Kim only compounds the problems of injuries; he makes the third who is off. So is Stephen Wicks. So is Mark Welford. If Grahame dances for Kim, someone must dance for Grahame, and so on. Life as usual.

Just as there are never enough dancers to go around, there is never enough space. Philip Prowse has commandeered the Opera Room, a slightly smaller studio than the Cranko Room, for a few hours of fittings and conferences. He is meeting today with Susanna Wilson, one of twelve freelance workers who have been engaged to make various costumes, helmets, headdresses and jewelry for *Lac*. Susanna has worked with Philip on other shows and she has already begun work on this one, proceeding as much from her initial discussions with him as from what she can actually see in his drawings. "I don't really like working with people whose work I don't know," says Philip. "You see, most designers don't show exactly what they want on the sketch. They give themselves a little leeway to change or revise later. I don't want to be bothered later, so I sketch exactly what I want. If someone you know says, 'Oh, this won't work,' you tend to listen to them because you trust them to know what they're talking about."

Samira Saidi, second cast to Anita Landa as the widowed Queen, mother of Prince Siegfried, has been called to this fitting and puts on whatever Susanna hands her. They consult her only as to its fit; otherwise, she could be a dressmaker's dummy. Their only concern is that Susanna execute Philip's idea, as expressed in his drawing, exactly as he saw it in his mind. Whether Sami actually likes what she is wearing is irrelevant, at least until she has to move in it onstage. At that point, months from now, Philip will say, "Dancers are so professional. If they object to something it's for a good reason, like they can't get their legs up. I love working in ballet." For now, no one's opinion matters but Peter Wright's, whose concept of the ballet the designs will help express.

"You said, 'Make her look like Queen Victoria,'" Susanna reminds Philip as she helps Sami dress, "so I thought I'd build a nice little bodice that would actually fit her and then build it up with quilting so that it's all part of the costume."

"Will there be any way she can leave it behind? You know, they hate to wear these things." He speaks from experience; he doesn't want his designs subjected to the dancers' whims. If he designs a costume, he wants to see it—all of it—on stage. "No," Susanna laughs, "it'll all be part of the same thing." He is after a particular shape, an hourglass. Seven hoops of whalebone in the underskirt, each wider in circumference than the one above, swell the topskirt like the base of a bell as it nears the floor. "No cloak," he points out, "but these long hanging sleeves, like a medieval sleeve pulled up. That'll help increase the width too."

They turn next to the sketches for the two ladies-in-waiting who escort the Queen Mother in the first and third acts. They do not dance; nevertheless, they have to be costumed. In rapid succession, Philip hands over samples of four black fabrics, two of them velvet, then black taffeta, and finally a black-based brocade. "They're in mourning, you see. Well, they're a bit less in mourning in Act 3, but you have to be very careful to balance it all, so you don't suddenly see something with a great spot of colour on it." He sums up all the shapes too: "They're all supposed to be medieval. The point is that it should look like *Lohengrin* done in 1860." That's it in a nutshell; that's what this production will look like. It is absolutely clear in his mind.

Taking notes at his elbow the whole time, supplying pins, swatches, names and measurements, is Kim Baker. She is in charge of coordinating the workers with both Philip and their supplies, of finding what he wants or coming up with something else if it can't be found, of remembering the questions that have to be asked of him and asking them. She is the stage manager for all the *Lac* costumes. One hundred and eight of them will apear on opening night, and she will oversee dozens more for the second and third casts. It is a mammoth job.

★   ★   ★

The numberless building that faces the stage door of the Royal Opera House is 45 Floral Street, home of administrative offices for the Opera House, its music library, workrooms for wardrobe, millinery, wigs and jewelry, and supplies and storage. The Pattern Room at the top of this building is the nerve centre of production wardrobe, Kim's domain. Perched on a high stool, Philip shuffles swatches as if they were cards and asks, "Do you think we could afford a complete fur cloak for the Master of Ceremonies? Right. I want that," handing over a sample of brown fur, "in black." Kim knows where the sample comes from, what it costs, whether it is still made, whether it is available in black. The fact that Philip wants it doesn't necessarily mean he can have it, but he certainly won't go without it for lack of trying on her part.

From a fistful of black and gold swatches she has provided, he selects one for a thin decorative border on Siegfried's Act 3 tunic, saying, "I'm sorry about this, but he *is* the Prince." The fabric is from Lanvin in Paris; it is not cheap. But it matches his vision of Siegfried in Act 3, and part of his job is to know his own mind and to make sure others get to know it too.

I am never to see Philip wearing anything but black, white and grey. He is a tall man, with the reedy, elegant build of a dancer and the soothing voice of a doctor. His hair and beard, although cropped short, appear both black and white. Today he wears a narrow black suit, a grey sweatshirt instead of a shirt, and another sweatshirt, this one white, knotted around his neck. His slim black moccasins and white socks are so invariable that they are practically invisible. He smokes constantly, and the chalk-blue package of his Gauloises shocks the eye each time it flashes in his hand.

September 14. Eleven weeks to opening night. Peter Wright's office is just a short stroll across the roof of Sadler's Wells from the Cranko Room, but it's often worlds away from the business of dancing. Four men gather one morning for a crucial, if hurried, production meeting. Peter arrives last. Moving with the lightness of the dancer he once was, he runs his hands quickly through his dark hair and sheds his formal business image with his sombre suit jacket. With two turns of his cuffs–subtly dark one day, sharply checked the next–he slips out of his administrative character and returns to the comfortable, shirtsleeve world of the theatre in which he has spent his life as performer, producer and director.

Jeffrey Phillips, one of the three already seated, is the production manager of the Royal Opera House. He is to props, paint and scenery construction what Kim Baker is to wardrobe: organizer, clearinghouse of information, central channel for questions and answers. Tom Walker is in charge of the Scenic Building unit, the construction shop where Philip's set will be built. John Hart is the company's Master Carpenter, who also coordinates the details of touring the set from one town to the next, setting it up and taking it down. Once it is built and delivered, he must maintain it and see that it functions.

Following the opening of *Swan Lake* in Manchester, the company will dance in eleven different theatres before its '81–'82 season ends. No two stages are the same size or shape. The question this morning is whether Philip's set will fit all of them. Before something is constructed which will then be found *not* to fit somewhere, every inch of stage depth, width and height must be considered. The office floor is blanketed with groundplans drawn to exact scale for exact reference. The four-way conversation goes like this:

"If you're talking about the actual dancing space, you're pretty shallow in Birmingham."

12

"The proscenium at Glasgow is a lot narrower than Birmingham, but the rest is all right."

"Stratford's going to be a bit narrow, a bit like a corridor."

"Well, we have to do it there," Peter mutters. "The old touring company used to do it. They love the classics."

"If you can do it in these other places, you can do it in Liverpool."

"Not much room on the prompt side in Eastbourne, but I think it's all right."

"There's no space at all on the OP side in Newcastle, about eight feet."

"What's there on the corner? A pub? A cafe? They've been talking about buying that shop for years." These four men know the corners of every stage around the country, the tight spots, the squeezes. They have to.

"Bournemouth you're in trouble with depth, and the grid height is nasty."

"Southampton's OK since they got rid of the bloody Cinemascope screen."

"Birmingham's the worst of the lot."

Why are they so worried about stage space? Philip's basic set is nothing more than six free-standing columns dressed with odd bits of furniture and a few props, which seems simple enough. But the columns just happen to be twenty feet high and a full metre square. Every inch in every direction on every stage will be crucial. You could, for example, fit either the set or the dancers on the stage at Sadler's Wells, but never both. The stage is no bigger than a pocket handkerchief, and the proscenium opening is only twenty-nine feet wide.

While they worry and debate, Philip focusses his attention on the most delicate of all his designs. In the Opera Room, he hovers solicitously over Galina's shoulder as the fitter kneels at her side, pinning the ice-white bodice of her Odette tutu to the broad spray of its skirt. Unfinished, the tutu seems all awkward corners, prickly with pins, and its flat wide topskirt is stiff as sugar icing. Galina knows she will look like a midget if the skirt is too long–in this case, too wide from edge to edge–for the length of her legs, but she doesn't say, "It must be shorter." Ballet is about manners, protocol, subtlety. With a small smile, all she says is "I'll have to grow longer legs."

"I found the most wonderful picture of Pavlova with Mordkin," Philip responds, "with the most lovely line in the tutu, sloping off from the bodice." He is assuring her, "Don't worry. It will fall more. It will be beautiful. In it you will look like, dance like, Anna Pavlova." Galina is not only Peter's co-producer, but the first cast Odette; as first among equal ballerinas, she is always treated with particular deference.

A rangy, bearded redhead looms momentarily over her strawberry-blonde topknot. Graham Crew, head of props, has brought the tambourines that will be used in the Neapolitan dance for Philip's approval. "If you don't like them, you don't have to have them, but they were incredibly cheap. They'd be absolutely ideal if the cymbals were gold instead of silver. Shall I just get some ribbon and tart them up? What kind of ribbon?"

Leaning her elbows on the rehearsal piano, Jean Percival waits her turn. The swan headdress she has made of pearls and white feathers winks and gleams against her soft flannel blouse; it is the prototype for all the corps swans. "They look so much better when you get them on a dancer. We do them on our heads, but they look different on a dancer's head." Galina tries her own on, and asks if the back can be more interesting, with longer feathers and a line that curls up away from her head. The swans will wear what they're given—it is not their place to have opinions—but Galina's opinion will be both sought and respected.

As she looks on a few days later, Philip supervises the fitting of the Mazurka dress: "I want the bosom padded underneath and slightly to the side." The fitter, Jean Hunniset, points out that this will make a shelf on top of the bust, "especially on a flat girl," and Galina has purposely chosen long slender girls for the Mazurka. "But they must be padded, rounded," he insists, curving his hands in a modified hourglass. "Not *too* much," cautions Galina. He has his designs firmly in mind, she the choreography—they will reach a good compromise.

He must also decide the colour of the shoes and tights for Benno and the waltz girls in Act 1 Kim reminds him, reading from a list that has no end. As fast as she crosses something off the top, she adds something else, another question, to the bottom. "And could the Czardas boot have a shaped heel, a Louis heel?" he asks her suddenly. "Because the costumes are so full, it has to be a straight boot for the girls, soft and laced up, with a two-inch heel like in *Raymonda*." She writes it down.

Pointe shoes drying

14

Boots and character shoes alone account for one-fifth of the entire costume budget for *Lac*; 150 pairs will be made for the production. Pointe shoes are another matter entirely and come out of another budget. Each girl is allotted ten pairs per month–twelve pairs for principals–not including dyed shoes, like the red ones in *Checkmate*. If a dancer wants or needs more shoes than that, she must buy them herself at roughly £10 per pair. "And *Lac*'ll be three pair a performance," one of them wails. "The whole thing's on pointe. You never come down."

Because they are so precious, you see shoes in dancers' hands nearly as often as on their feet. Ribbons and elastic must constantly be stitched on new pairs, shoe polish and surgical spirit dabbed on old ones to erase all but the blackest smudges. To take the shine off new pointe shoes so they'll blend smoothly with the pale pink of their tights, the girls pat the pink satin with the same body make-up, called wet-white, that they apply to themselves for *Sylphides* and *Swan Lake*. To stiffen the toes for greater support and longer wear, they shellac the canvas inner lining two or three times a week, and then prop the shoe up to dry on a radiator or in the hotbox that dries the pin-curled wigs. Briar Brownson, the "shoe lady" who tours with them, carries about thirty pairs of spare pointe shoes for each woman in the company and six pairs each of black and white slippers for every man. If her stock falls any lower than that, she begins to get very nervous.

While she's stitching ribbons on her pointe shoes over lunch in the canteen, Sami Saidi tells me she and Derek Purnell have just done the great *pas de deux* from the second act of *Lac* for a lecture-demonstration. "It was marvellous because Desmond (Kelly) taught it to us. It was like having private coaching sessions. I'm sure Marion (Tait) and Maggie (Barbieri) will have that, but the rest of us–I'm about eighth cast, I'll probably never get to do it–just have to watch and listen and try to learn it on our own. For the demonstration, we kept doing a bit and then tacking a bit on after it and then going back to the beginning again. I never realized how exhausting it is, just the *pas de deux*. And all I was working on was the technique. It really makes you appreciate the details, the artistry really, that go into the whole thing. I didn't even start on the where-you-look and when-you-look and how you give the illusion of being a swan. I had enough with just the technique."

Derek is slightly more matter-of-fact. "You'd have a hard time getting through the (Royal Ballet) School without running into *Lac*. You'd have bits of it in repertory class, and the boys have *pas de deux* class three or four times a week, so you'd have it there too. And I did second act with Pippa Wylde from the main company, not for graduation, just for a School performance." It's like saying "We're not quite starting from scratch," but of course they are, even the older and more experienced of them.

Desmond Kelly, who is also sitting in the canteen, pulls a mock-desperate face as he announces he hasn't even started work yet on Rothbart. A principal dancer and the company's ballet master, he will be dancing both Siegfried and Rothbart by turns. "There's no respect nowadays," he grumbles as they laugh at his plight, but then adds more seriously, "When I was young, you didn't take your place at the barre or in the centre until the principals had arranged themselves. And you didn't speak to them unless they spoke to you." The formality of those days has all but disappeared from their world, and the new informality between principals and corps dancers breeds a closeness on stage which the company will have to fight in *Swan Lake*. The nineteenth-century classics are as much about rank and hierarchical structures, within daily society and within the more sealed society of the Imperial ballet, as they are about swans and magic. What the senior dancers bring to the company–and they know it and the company knows it–is their own real experience of "one's place" in a formal world and of the "proper way" of doing things. When Anita Landa, their ballet mistress, makes her first entrance in Act 1 as the grieving Queen Mother, even in her street clothes and high-heeled shoes she is dignity personified, so at home in a position of authority that what is convincing to her audience convinces the youngsters in the studio as well and offers them an example of grandeur by which they can measure their own.

As we leave the table, one boy says to another, "I'll do you tonight and you do Mark. Mark has to do John." They're now short another boy; Bintley is off with a swollen knee. No one can afford to be injured for long. Although muscles remember for years what they have learned to do, they very rapidly lose the strength to do it, and "getting back" is a long, arduous struggle. But dropping out of competition, even briefly, hurts them more than their damaged tendons and ligaments do. For all their friendliness, competition between the dancers is fierce, subtle perhaps but steady. Not everyone will dance all the time, and they all know it. The moment they leave the protective atmosphere of the School for the professional one of the company, they sprout radar for criticism, even unspoken. They develop a sense of urgency about time and opportunity, always present, always passing. Their eyes work overtime; they watch themselves, their colleagues and their teachers–Peter, Galina, Desmond, Alain, Anita, and their *régisseur*, Ronald Plaisted–who all peer back impassively.

Nicola Katrak, twenty years old and clearly on the rise, is scowling before the Act 1 *pas de quatre* rehearsal in the Cranko Room. "I'm annoyed because I can't turn. I've got a thing about it in my mind, and I know everyone's watching it." All the dancers tend to magnify their shortcomings this way, even as they concentrate on correcting them, because someone is always watching, judging, choosing. Who will be singled out for larger parts, more noticeable work? Who will fade further into the crowd, further from the shining footlights?

It is all on their minds and in the air, always, but you cannot see it when they start to work, flurrying behind Peter. He choreographs on his feet, trying things out, demonstrating, adjusting a hand or the tilt of an ankle. Choreographing, he forgets he is not still a dancer; he performs what he can, and gestures flamboyantly for the rest.

The dance he is making is a small entertainment for Prince Siegfried, offered him by his friend Benno and two girls. Each girl extends a hand to the Prince to include him, and then jumps away from him with a small springy *pas de chat*. "Not that courtly," Peter instructs, "and not that peasanty. A bit of the gypsy . . ." They do the phrase at the same time but on opposite sides of the Prince and in opposite directions. The next phrase takes them both in the same direction in a circle of *jetés*—one of them jumps as the other lands. Nikki and Christine Aitken count half-aloud, moving very fast. It is, in all, ten bars of music, and each of the two phrases is called a "step" although it is actually made up of several individual steps of the classical vocabulary. So the ten bars comprise the "first step" and the "second step" together; in order to finish the *jeté* phrase at the right time, they count what they have to do as 8, then 6, then 10.

They assume nothing. Which arm does Peter want up, over their heads, and which to the hip? He says "It's nice when you make them very definite. Right up on the *jeté* and then open way back. And of course we'll have *pas de chat* with both feet up"—tucked up high underneath them—"and maybe holding the skirt? Yes? Now let's make that first bit more interesting," which also means harder. The dancers wait for him to think and tread immediately on his thoughts, expanding and completing the move as soon as he speaks or sketches it. He takes this simultaneous translation for granted—"But it's easy in this because it's all classical," the girls agree. "What you must do next just comes naturally"—and relies on them as well to remember everything they did "yesterday," which is not yesterday, of course, but whenever they were last called to rehearse this dance.

In another, more crowded studio, Debbie Chapman, the company's choreologist, is in charge, notated score in hand. Although they've all tried, no one—dancer or rehearsal coach—has yet figured out how to be in two places at the same time. As a result, every day's rehearsal schedule poses massive logistical problems, which are compounded for *Lac* by the fact that Ron, Anita, Galina . . . every rehearsal authority except Peter . . . is also appearing *in* the production. Debbie's score is more accurate than most people's memories, and her authority is never questioned. Aided by both, she will rehearse three separate numbers today: the Act 1 waltz, which is a divertissement by four couples of the Prince's friends; the *pas de six* for three couples which opens the ballroom festivities in Act 3; and finally the solo variations for the three Princesses who are invited to the grand reception to meet and possibly marry the Prince. "They can hardly find three princesses from different countries," Galina jokes one day. "Of course they can't, darling," Philip quips back. "Everyone has been turned into a swan."

Watching the grip and shift of the waltz couples' hands, you begin to see the art and science of partnering. Two people supporting one another can do things that one alone would find physically impossible. Choreographers know this and capitalize on it, but it is up to the dancers to make the just-this-side-of-impossi-

ABOVE Act 1 waltz

LEFT Marking the
Spanish Dance

18

ble combinations of movements work. Who grabs whom and when? Who pushes where? Their collaboration must be rehearsed. Tiny adjustments must be made, as partners or steps change, as someone loses weight or gains a bulky costume. Peter wants the bodies to look a certain way. The dancers keep pushing toward that look all the time, and, if the movements can be done, he will get what he wants. But then they must work out, very slowly and with precise calculations of space and timing and balance of weight, how to do it, smoothly, repeatedly, again and again.

Peter rehearses the Polacca, which ends Act 1 with six gentlemen of the court and the four boys from the preceding waltz pacing off stately formations. The boys must forget phrases of eight counts as fast as Peter shapes new ones, forget and remember without hesitation. And faced with the bright, ordinary room and the motley-clothed, familiar bodies, Peter must retain a vision of the mood and style he wants the boys to express, and see it clearly enough that he can make them see it. He cocks his head, and all ten boys tailor their energy so their torsoes dip at the same angle.

At the end of the day, the quartet who will dance the Neapolitan divertissement in Act 3 rehearse from memory what Peter has already set—which is most of the dance. The two boys have tambourines, as they will onstage, and so do two extra casts, another four boys, who are watching and working in miniature behind them. Since rehearsal time is at a premium, common sense dictates that you watch any number you may eventually have to perform as often as you can lay your eyes on it. Throughout these weeks, extra dancers will fringe the central action of every rehearsal, flicking their fingers, shifting their weight from one foot to the other, learning. They call it "marking." You see every dance in duplicate, triplicate, every time the music plays. "It's good to have it go through your body," they say.

Questions arise about this dance before the four-bar musical introduction ends: Was it this count or that, did I say this arm or the other? And the noise is deafening, all the boys with tambourines, all the girls—three casts, six girls, twelve feet flying—all the jumping, and Peter shouting and clapping and stamping out the rhythm. The room, the dance, is a whirlwind, and it is the Ballet Room, small, irregularly shaped, with mirrors on more than four sides because of the jogs in the walls. One is surrounded by Neapolitans and tambourines. They keep dancing, faster, on command, past what seems possible.

The fact that the dancers continue to look fresh is an illusion. They are actually exhausted nearly all the time, but they continually change into fresh practice clothes.

September 21. Ten weeks to opening night. When the company leaves London for Plymouth, where they will perform in a huge canvas tent called the Big Top, even the administrative offices are closed and locked. Management tours too because, new production or no, the daily business of running, organizing and maintaining a company must continue. While staging the new *Lac*, Peter

Wright must also fulfill his obligations as Artistic Director, overseeing the company's health, wealth and future plans. He must also speak on its behalf to the Opera House administration, which holds final approval over any plans he may make and over the budget with which he will turn them into reality. Peter's personal assistant, Alison Palmer, and the touring assistant, Clare Temple, travel in order to juggle the minutia of meetings, rehearsal schedules, casting changes, press appointments and performance notes. Christopher Nourse, the General Manager, whose duties are financial and organizational, goes too.

No one is left behind but the injured, who can't dance, and the production staff, whose concerns lie elsewhere. Sitting in the Pattern Room with one hand resting on the constantly ringing telephone and the other scribbling on a yellow memo pad, Kim Baker names some of those concerns.

"What have we got in this show?" she asks rhetorically. "Well, for example, we have three court officials in Act 1 wearing "walk-on costumes"—they don't dance. Philip has designed cloaks for them that are five metres square, which must be padded, appliquéd, and have three rows of braid put on." You haven't really got *Swan Lake* if you leave out the splendour. Or, as Philip put it somewhat later, "The nineteenth-century pieces are the Fabergé of dance, gold Easter eggs covered in lapis lazuli—quite pointless, but there it is. Those ballets belonged to the nineteenth-century context. They were part of the business of having an Imperial Russian court, and they must reflect that fact. They have no relevance now—and it's an abomination to try to give them relevance— but they are never presented in their full panoply."

And where does the panoply come from? "Apart from Marjorie Rogers and Jane Cowood, who will make all the tutus," says Kim, "we're also using three costume workrooms in the house, and the swan headdresses are being made here." She digresses a minute on tutus, not as open-and-closed a subject as you might expect. Each of the four ladies who will dance the dual role of Odette-Odile—Samsova, Tait, Barbieri and Sherilyn Kennedy—will have three tutus; one black for Act 3, and a fresh crisp white one for both Act 2 *and* Act 4. "Odette should never have to put a cold, wet, dirty tutu on again to dance Act 4," Kim explains. The arithmetic is then simple: three tutus apiece for four ladies equals an even dozen principals' tutus. The arithmetic is even simpler for the rest of the swans' tutus. Excluding the four Odettes, there are twenty-five ladies in the company, so twenty-five swan tutus will be made, one to fit each of them. Peter's choreography may only require a corps of twelve, two solo swans and four cygnets, but casting will change frequently—even daily if injuries intrude— and sooner or later, every last girl in the company will appear somewhere on that stage as a swan. No one doubts it for a moment. Given the inevitable reshuffling, it would be foolhardy *not* to make every girl a tutu now. "Did you know Peter originally wanted the cygnets in black for the last act?" Kim's face reflects horror at the mere thought of the wardrobe confusion.

"Casting is always a problem for us. There are nine people covering Benno,

Kim Baker

and nine Princes cast in all, four active and five to come. And there are twelve girls covering the four places in the Czardas. Lili Sobieralska, who's in charge of running wardrobe, says she needs eight completed costumes to cover the range of sizes. If you make only four, with huge plackets to account for the different waists, Peter complains that the hems are different lengths."

As she itemizes who will make what, the list of people who have to consult Philip grows and grows. She mentions Jennifer Adey in millinery, Ron Freeman in wigs and Nesta Brown, whose tiny office and supply room of pointe shoes is behind the stage at Covent Garden: "She must confirm what he meant when he said 'a Louis heel.' There are three types of Louis heel she can order for him.

"We have tights in stock and we can dye them, but all the fabrics are being ordered to colour. The range of colour has been cut by one-third in the first and third acts because he's decided on so much black. Philip doesn't like to dye, paint or spray in after the fabric has been cut and sewn, so we must have a huge range of samples to choose from, because he gets his choice from the fabrics, just as they are." The phone shrills again. "Everyone expected to start cutting a month ago," she concludes, snatching up the receiver, "but we haven't ordered the fabric yet."

No fabric? No activity in the workrooms either. For the time being, very few ripples anywhere on this *Lac*.

September 28. Nine weeks to opening night. Lucky I spoke to Kim when I did; from today, she will not have a moment to spare. The Sadler's Wells Royal Ballet has just received final approval for its proposed new production of *Swan Lake.* "If you tell us the name of the production and of the designer, we can give you an estimate of our budget almost to the pound," Kim told me last week, and that's exactly what she's been doing ever since.

In the fiscal year 1980–'81, the cost to the Sadler's Wells Royal Ballet of paying fees (as opposed to salaries), producing new works, and refurbishing old ones came to £88,988. Staging ballets is an enormously expensive undertaking. Even with the aid of private sponsorship, which *Swan Lake* will receive from the Royal Opera House Trust and an anonymous source, every decision hinges as much on its financial feasibility as on its artistic desirability. After close and serious debate, the Opera House administration has decided that *Swan Lake* has both.

An all but audible sigh of relief hangs over 45 Floral Street. Elbow deep in lists and schedules, Jose Phillips, the company's press officer, is beaming. "It would have put us back two to three years with the public to cancel this production. Especially in Birmingham where we're opening a renovated theatre, after *Jesus Christ Superstar,* and have sold the subscription on the basis of *Swan Lake.*" Coloured brochures litter her desk for Manchester, Birmingham, Leeds . . . all the cities and theatres in which the company has already announced its lavish new production. They will not be disappointed.

If the dancers have known the production was in doubt, they certainly aren't talking about it in Plymouth. Once they leave London, more pressing and immediate problems claim their attention, like where to live. Many people return to the digs they found on previous tours, and, depending on the city, a lucky few go home to their families. Rooms near the theatre are prized, as are central heating, freely offered hot water, and the possibility of a meal after the show. When you're staying in digs, you've got to decide if you're more tired or more hungry after a performance. If you can find a café or restaurant that stays open late enough to feed you, and if you can keep awake long enough to eat, you may not be able to get back to your room. If you go straight home on a late bus or in a car that's going your way, you may go to bed hungry. But there are other priorities too: "We all stay quite a way out of Plymouth," says Bess Dales. "It's too much like an extension of work if we live nearby. And to have a cottage, with a private beach, miles from anywhere . . . Wouldn't *you* rather?"

The dancer's world is eternally the same; only the details change. Peter Wright recalls that the first time he toured, which was with Ballets Jooss, he was in Wolverhampton just after the War. "Everything was rationed. Digs were hard to find. What I found cost 17s. 6d. for full board, but I had to share a bed– one of those beds that's collapsed in the middle–with the assistant stage manager, who had very smelly feet. And it was so cold and wet that the condensation was running down the walls inside the room, and we had to drag the bed into the middle of the room to stay dry. Coal was rationed, so we could only put

Christine Aitken and Peter Wright in the Hope Baptist Church hall

one piece on the fire at a time. And the landlady was drunk all the time and gave us fish and chips for every meal. And I thought it was all wonderful."

While the Big Top offers the dancers a chance to perform for 1200 people a night on twice as big a stage as the Wells', it is still a canvas tent. In Plymouth, it is damp and cold, and erected miles from anything useful–you walk for fifteen minutes without passing a single shop or restaurant. And it is raining. The dressing rooms, showers, toilets, wardrobe, and offices are strung out in a parade of caravans fitted end to end like a long, well-lit tunnel. But the canteen is outside the warm enclosure, in another tent the size of a small room. Wooden planks keep the folding tables and chairs out of the mud; the rain comes in the slits of the canvas and laps at the planks. The dancers buy their tea and slabs of cheese and pieces of fruit, and carry them back to their dressing rooms, where it is at least dry. They wrap their feet in plastic bags to protect their pointe shoes from the soggy planks.

There is no proper classroom or rehearsal room, and the stage alone can't accommodate all the rehearsing. So, for the week, the company has hired the meeting hall of the Hope Baptist Church for a few hours every day. It is simply an oblong room, thirty feet square, one storey high, with a basketball hoop minus its net at one end and a small stage–a platform, really, with a velvet curtain in front of it–at the other end; the stage serves as a changing room. There is no mirror. During their entire stay in Plymouth and most of the time they are on tour, the dancers will not be able to see the adjustments they make when they are told to correct themselves. They must carry a complete image of the way they look, modified sometimes by fractions of inches, in their heads. Try it; assume a position, any position, and then try recreating it twenty-four hours later. You might not even be able to remember it, much less reproduce it. Dancers do both, every day, and are severely and repeatedly criticized by their teachers and then by the press if they fail. "I couldn't see myself. There was no mirror" is no excuse. There are no excuses.

Margaret Barbieri spends an hour with Peter practicing nothing but Odette's Act 2 solo. "I was in the old touring company when we used to do *Lac*, but I was only in the corps then. I've done just a few performances of Odette before, in Frankfurt, so I know a different solo. It's really harder that way than not knowing it at all." Muscles have a memory of their own which can outlast the mind's. If a dancer panics or blanks, he will often revert, quite unconsciously, to something he danced years earlier, forgetting the steps he rehearsed that very afternoon and has been perfecting for the last several months. He will find himself in the wrong position on stage, miles away from his partner, moving to the wrong music. It can happen.

Lili Griffiths, Sandra Madgwick, Ann Carol and Lynne Wake would probably never have learned another version of the cygnets dance even if they were older and more experienced, because it is generally accepted as one of the few surviving pieces of the original ballet. Well known move by move to audiences around the world, the tiniest slip will be noticed, not least of all because the four dancers perform exactly the same steps at the same time throughout the dance, with their arms crisscrossed before them and all their hands clasped. They must cover a great deal of the stage in a very short time, they may not drop hands until the final two counts, even their heads must move in tandem. And the tempo is very quick and the steps are very small and neat, tiny jumps and beats. They are winded after running it through once, as if they had sprinted three blocks for a moving bus. And simply doing it is not enough–they must do it right.

Galina: "The heads on the *échappés* go down, to the side, to the front, to the side."

Peter: "And you must turn out on the *petits jetés* at the end. You can't do them with your knee facing down."

Galina: "When you come on and take hands, you're facing front with the leg *croisé* behind you. No, *you're* not *croisé*–the leg is *croisé*."

Peter: "And you're *all* princesses changed to swans, so you must be very proud, very classical." And dance up to tempo and remember your heads and don't drop your hands. They do it for nearly an hour.

Cygnets. (left to right) Lili Griffiths, Petal Miller, Ann Carol, Sandra Madgwick

Class on stage the next morning seems even more silent and concentrated than usual in the vast empty tent. Only the work lights are on. The rain pours down the canvas. The dancers sweat. You notice the mirror's absence even more than in rehearsal. Corrections are made by ear instead of by eye.

Immediately afterwards there is a fifteen-minute call for the Mazurka in Act 3. It seems to be a brush-up rehearsal, just to refresh the memory and open the dance onto the stage after the cramped space of the rehearsal room. Rather than trying to put what she wants into words, Galina simply demonstrates her corrections. The dancers, especially the girls, mimic her as exactly as possible–she is the real thing.

By the time they are finished, all the rest of the girls have arrived. The next hour and a half is down on the callsheet for Act 4, which hasn't been finished yet, and everyone wears a practice tutu. There's no point placing reed-thin swans around the stage in pretty patterns. In a leotard, each girl takes no more space than the width of her slim hips; in a tutu, each girl fills a space more than a yard across. The mismatched tutus drip torn rosettes and bedraggled ribbon, but no one notices or cares. They are not costumes now, only measurements of space, purely functional and nothing else.

They begin just before "the storm," not the storm that seems to sound in the music but the one that Peter has written into his libretto, a storm that the evil magician Rothbart whips up in "a vain attempt" to prevent Siegfried from

25

Act 4. Corps de ballet

finding Odette. "What are *they* doing," Peter asks Debbie Chapman, pointing to one group of swans, "while they're doing *that*?" pointing to a second group and sketching a step with his hands. Watching them resurrect what he did the last time, he says to Desmond, "I think I want to introduce Rothbart up there on the centre rostrum in the storm." Every move they execute helps him find what is in his mind by showing him an alternative. Without looking quite right to him, a step or pose can still look very definitely wrong. Every change he makes guides the dancers closer to what he imagines them doing.

Having completed Act 4 up to Siegfried's entrance, they go back to the beginning of the act to run it straight through . . . and stop right away over the spacing of the dancers and the speed of their arm movements. When they enter, they form two groups facing upstage—away from the audience—and offstage, which means that they cannot see one another. Peter won't let them turn their heads to look at the girl alongside of them, so they must gauge their position from the girl in front of them, who they follow on and stand behind. If one girl is in the wrong place, every swan behind her, coming downstage, will be wrong and so will the shape of the whole group. The *port de bras* itself is not hard either, just a slow, mournful wave as if they're looking through the trees for their queen. But they don't wave on every note of the music, and they still can't see each other. Will they keep together better if they use fast counts—1,2,3,4—or half counts—1-and-2-and-3-and-4? Finally, all eighteen swans turn to face Peter, Debbie Chapman, Anita Landa, and Desmond, who are ranged in straight chairs along the footlights, and they mark the movements together, singing the counts

26

aloud. Hilary Bell, the company pianist, squashes her cigarette in the discarded pointe shoe she's using for an ashtray, and thumps the melodies out of the old, upright piano, singing with them.

Slowly and with difficulty they stumble through to the end of the dance, with the same problem of counts interfering all along the way. When they finish, Peter says flatly, "That was kind of awful," which, judging from their set, drawn faces, doesn't tell them anything they don't already know. The last time they repeat it, they all seem to have their eyes closed.

But "everyone's really pleased to be doing this *Lac*," one of them tells me in the dressing room. "It's a really prestigious resident-company thing to do, and we always feel sort of second-best. And there are so many numbers in it to work on and really dance in. Even if you're just a swan, you feel you're working on something good and it feels good on your body."

All too conscious of the technical and dramatic challenges *Swan Lake* holds, the principals are greedy for rehearsal and grasp at every suggestion gratefully. Carl Myers and Sherilyn Kennedy are in the hall and ready to begin work when Peter arrives. They have danced together often, but the give-and-take of every *pas de deux* needs rehearsing no matter how familiar the partners. Without constant practice, a man can hold a woman too tightly or not tightly enough, stand too close to give her proper support or too far away. She can jump without pushing enough and he will be lifting dead-weight; she can push in a direction he doesn't expect and fly out of his hands. Although Sherilyn and Carl don't discuss it, they know too, deep down, that the *pas de deux* in Acts 2 and 3 of *Lac* are two of the most important setpieces of the entire classical repertory, yardsticks by which entire careers are measured.

Sherilyn, who has danced in the company for six years, has only been a principal for one. "I didn't want to do *Swan Lake*, not at all. I'd rather do *any* of the

Madeleine Sheehan and Galina Samsova

others–*Beauty* I know I could do. But then Marion went off and I *had* to do it. It just fell on me. I've only seen it once, and I've never been in it at all, not even as a swan. I don't feel comfortable in it, Act 2 especially, and there are so many people telling you different things. I did ask Galina: 'Now, tell me exactly. When I come on, am I a swan or what?' And she said, 'Oh, you're a woman but still with the characteristics of a swan.' Well, I don't know how to do that, be like a swan. And of course with a new role you've got so much to do to remember it all that you can't think about the little things. Peter's always been on at me about using my arms better, so of course that's the first thing I *don't* do right."

Peter reminds her to lengthen her line by stretching her arms fully in every position. He debates with Carl whether to support her with one hand or two as she hops down what will be a diagonal of swans. Nothing escapes his notice. Having warmed up on the Act 2 *pas de deux*, they go straight on to Act 3. Sherilyn perches confidently in *piquée arabesque*, leaning against thin air, and

Black Swan *pas de deux*. (left to right) Sherilyn Kennedy and Carl Myers, Galina Samsova and David Ashmole. At far right, *régisseur* Ronald Plaisted

whispers to a non-existent Rothbart. Seconds later, they are totally confused, all confidence evaporated. Carl and Peter know different versions. Galina has taught things and then changed them, and Sherilyn can't remember what to remember and what to forget. They search each others' eyes hopefully, as if the right steps will suddenly leap out, but they are stuck. They cannot go forward, so they go back. Hilary plays, and the Black Swan *pas de deux* begins yet again.

Plymouth is beginning to tell on them, the cold, the floor in the church hall, which is probably concrete under the vinyl surface that has been laid, the distance they have to travel to the theatre . . ."I think it's damaging," says Margaret, who has pulled a groin muscle. The medical report is mixed. Sami Saidi has a bursa on her Achilles tendon and can't do any pointe work: "I can't even point my foot. It's like some dead thing, flopping on the end of my leg." Kim Reeder is still off, but Stephen Wicks is dancing again. Iain Webb has flu but is still on. Chenca Williams and June Highwood are back in class. The plaster has come off Marion's foot. Michael Corder has left the company, so a body must be found to dance where he used to. Two students from the Royal Ballet School, Gillian Maclaurin and Russell Maliphant, have arrived to make up the proper numbers. Hilary calls it "the week of the bad piano."

The three-couple Czardas is allotted fifteen minutes after class in the church hall. Dancers stack up like dominoes, three casts rehearsing in each couple's stage position. It is impossible to distinguish the first cast from the second or third, and you cannot tell who is dancing and who is marking. The second time, Hilary and Stephen Lade play four-hand piano to counter the noise. After the third runthrough, Galina leaves and a full company call for *Papillon* claims the precious space and most of the afternoon.

Late in the day, Peter works for an hour and a half with as many of the *Lac* principals as can be collected, primarily Galina and her partner David Ashmole, with Desmond as Rothbart. By watching and listening, he will learn Siegfried while he actually rehearses Rothbart, as will Alain Dubreuil who will eventually play both roles too. Galina wears her street clothes; Margaret and Sherilyn, dressed to dance, stay upstage of her, echoing every movement.

If the set will allow it, Peter wants to run Acts 1 and 2 together, with a short pause for the scene shift but no interval. He now decides that Rothbart must be onstage at the start of the second act, first crumpled among the leaves on the upstage platform and then slowly rising like someone coming out of the earth. The audience will see him at once and, when the Prince enters, he will immediately sense something ominous about the place. But deciding all that is one thing and determining which music Rothbart should move on takes considerably longer. When should he move? For how long should he move? Should he come down off the platform? Should Siegfried see him or only sense him? Peter only stabs at the questions, putting them into Desmond's head and Galina's and Alain's for further consideration, and then goes on to the expository scene in which Siegfried and Odette converse in formal mime.

Act 2. Galina Samsova and David Ashmole

It should be quite straightforward, but in fact, no one really remembers all the details of the mime or knows exactly how to adjust them for this production. They are all thinking on their feet, pooling different versions from different generations and different companies—the Royal Ballet, Festival, Stuttgart, Zurich, Frankfurt, Kiev. Even Peter has danced in *Swan Lake*.

This rehearsal is not about old gestures in old stories, but about making clear and logical sense of things for the dancers and for the audience. "You have to take *Swan Lake* very, very seriously; it's about a very serious subject," Peter has cautioned. "I always have to divorce myself from those preconceived ideas, start on clean soil. I always have to make a dramatic line, a sort of graph, a shape, that I really believe in. It's not at all hard with *Swan Lake*—it's all there for you."

They change the moment where Siegfried picks up his crossbow to shoot and Odette leans over him in *arabesque*. Galina says, "It happens at the end of the act

30

anyway, just before I *bourrée* off, and it always looks here as if he's going to shoot *her*, not Rothbart." Instead of risking her life, Odette will remind Siegfried that if Rothbart is killed, his spell over her can never be broken. Galina leans on David's outstretched arm, gesturing mournfully toward Rothbart's ominous figure, and then slips sadly away. Peter adds later, "You use what you've got around you. If Galina hadn't been in the company, I don't know if I'd have gone rushing off to find her. But I knew she was essential to this production after seeing her work on *Paquita*. Her background and knowledge . . . I knew she could give the production something I never could. It's a gift to work with her."

October 5. Eight weeks to opening night. Following the production during the next three weeks is like trying to track individual drops in a massive waterfall. The production staff in London pours out its skill and energy, and hats, chairs, shoes, windows, dresses and tiaras appear where nothing had existed but fabric, wire, wood, paint and black and white drawings. When all the work finally cascades together, on the stage of the Palace Theatre in Manchester, the drops will unite, like the brushstrokes in a painting, into the realization of Philip's scenic and costume designs. Every day now, more instructions and supplies trickle out of Kim Baker's Pattern Room and Jeffrey Phillips' Model Room, and more hands lift to transform them. Time channels the on-rushing efforts; the less of it there is, the faster everyone must work.

RIGHT Spanish costume: sketch and sleeve

FAR RIGHT Leaf carpet for Act 2 and 4

In the Model Room, under the eaves at 55 Floral Street, Jeffrey mentions in passing that a new production of Gluck's *Alceste* will open at the Royal Opera House on Wednesday, November 26, the night before *Lac* opens in Manchester. It is a decisive factor in the *Lac* preparations, affecting everyone except the dancers, but he states it as a plain fact: "It might make things a bit difficult, but they *can* be done."

Philip's set is massive, dark, and relatively simple, consisting almost entirely of the six enormous columns. For Act 1, a courtyard of the palace, a platform and balustrade will stand upstage centre and complete the scene. For the moonlit lakeside in Acts 2 and 4, the balustrade will disappear and a canvas throw appliquéd with leaves will cover the stairs, blending them into the black and silver backdrop, standing flats and hanging borders. Peter confides long after

Designer's model: Ac
3 backdrop

opening night that "people were shocked by the designs, so dark and austere. 'People in the provinces will be so upset,' they said. 'They want to see that lovely blue lake and those lovely trees. They'll be so disappointed.' Well, no one's been the least disappointed."

Philip has chosen gold and red for the court scene, and the Act 3 backdrop must be fitted with a window in which the vision of Odette will appear. Two imposing thrones and some high-backed gold chairs will partially mask the black and silver columns, as will red banners hanging from the invisible rafters of the great hall and a red-gold carpet covering the central staircase. "It's a marvellous basic set," beams Peter, "that can be changed by rearranging things like staircases and furniture–that's the genius of Prowse. It's virtually the same set all the way through, so you needn't have long intervals doing enormous scene changes."

From Jeffrey's viewpoint, everything begins with the model of the set, which Philip delivered to him–painted, textured and constructed to an exact one to twenty-five scale–late in May. From that model, dimensional drawings have been made, indicating the size and shape, the "what" of all the set's pieces. These have gone to Tom Walker, the chief carpenter, who will himself make the con-structional drawings, depicting the "how" of the set's construction, and pass them on to the carpenters in his shop. Jeffrey has sent Philip's scale drawings of the backcloths, banners and cut-out branches that overhang the lake to Robin Snow, who is in charge of the paint shop. The prop shop in Killick Street will take care of the smaller pieces, but everyone there is too busy to deal with *Swan Lake* just yet. Props is usually responsible for anything a dancer carries onstage– a stool, a crossbow, a tambourine–but if the object is actually worn, like a crown or a fan, it is considered a costume. If it is so large and heavy that the stagehands must move it and set it on stage, it is probably scenery, but the rules are not hard and fast. So long as everything that will eventually be needed is made, no one minds too much who actually makes it or where.

★   ★   ★

In the East End, nearly in Stepney, stands an old cinema with a blank marquee. Once the Roxy Cinema, now the London Opera Centre, it houses the Opera House's own paint studio, a huge, oblong room measuring ninety feet by fifty feet. The scenic artists work under the supervision of Robin Snow, who is white-haired and as puckish with good humour as a large man can be. He intro-duces himself and his work like this: "I'm sixty-five this January. The staff here is two scenic artists, myself, and a labourer. Two weeks ago we got designs for the branches for *Swan Lake*, last week we got designs for the banners, this morn-ing the Act 3 backcloth. There's plenty of work to do."

He explains that in English opera houses there is usually a paint frame behind or above the stage, on which work is hung. On the continent, however, the tradition is to work "on the floor" as they are doing here; the particular bit of floor they're using, which runs the entire width of the room, was originally the back of the cinema stalls. Rob's preference for the floor is obvious; he likes painting "wet," leaning against a firm backing, using a brush on a stick "just for the practice, because you never stop learning, do you?" His assistant Mike feels exactly the same. The combination of a ladder and a distancing glass gives them an overall view of their careful handiwork. The ladder is actually a little platform with a railing on it at the top of an eight-foot flight of steps—if you're smart, you take the glass up with you to save running extra stairs. The glass puts you forty feet back, like the view through the wrong end of your binoculars. With a cloth that's fifty feet by twenty-four feet as the Sadler's Wells cloths are, you need some distance just to see what you've been doing.

They must approach every piece of every show in a different way. For example, you can paint all the banners you want to onto one huge canvas and then cut them out to the proper shape and size. But once you've drawn the window for the vision onto the Act 3 backcloth, you must *not* cut it out until all the work on that canvas is completed—the painting, spraying and appliqué—or the cloth will buckle. The window will hang on the same batten as the cloth, but it will only be perfectly aligned with the space you leave for it if you go to the carpenter's shop, draw the window he is building, and then transfer your own drawing and measurements onto your canvas. The layout and irregular pattern of the Act 2 branches is transferred from the drawing another way. First you photocopy the designer's original scale drawing and square the photocopy so that each square represents one square metre. Then you mark your canvas in one metre squares and, by hand and eye, transfer to the canvas what appears in each square of the drawing.

Painting provides just as many choices or variables. After the Act 3 banners were dyed cranberry red, Mike mottled the even dye with black, reproducing the shapes and blotches on Philip's tiny model banners. Then they were sprayed red and black, and dappled with gold paint last of all. The edges began fraying as soon as they were cut out, so every raw edge was thickened with a double layer of paint, front and back.

The banners present a flat surface, but the third-act backcloth will have a textured one, which the scenic artists will create by ruching up lightweight muslin and gluing it to the canvas backing. They spray every inch of the muslin bright orange first; if they bunched it up, glued it on and *then* sprayed it, they'd be touching up the original pale muslin with orange paint every time a loose fold came away from the backing.

"No one tells us how to do it," Rob says proudly. "We have to sort it out for ourselves. We use rollers a lot for texturing, combs, rakes, garden sprayers—you couldn't use *them* on the frame. You might think this brush is worn out. Well, it is, but you can use it for wood-graining." They stick cork or mica chips to canvas for texture, or twisted net or a thick sprinkling of flock, but only on up-

LEFT Brushes and rollers

BELOW Tom Walker and Frank
Kirby

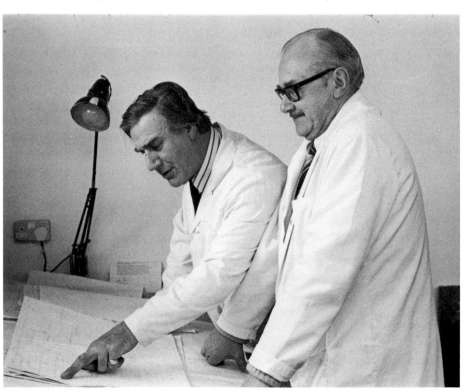

right flats, never on backdrops. Once canvas is thickened with texture, and thickened irregularly at that, it will neither roll nor fold, which means it won't tour well. Which means the Sadler's Wells Royal Ballet can't use it.

Nor can they use scenery that won't tour, as I learn in the carpentry shop, appropriately called the Old Vic Annexe, which huddles in the vast shadow of Waterloo Station and in the smaller, already fading one of the Old Vic Theatre. Tom Walker and his chief assistant, Frank Kirby, preside over its calm order. Tom has thick, wavy grey hair and a round grinning face; you could see him as a publican or a policeman. Frank, slightly bald and with his remaining hair cropped close, smokes a pipe and peers placidly through his glasses. His fingers are extraordinarily clean. Both men—and the eight carpenters and two semi-skilled labourers in their shop—wear white lab coats. Tom and Frank have worked together for twenty-six years. Not surprisingly, they finish each other's thoughts. "He knows more about me than my wife does," says Frank. "He's spent more time with me."

"The exercise with scenery," says Tom, leaning back in his chair, "is to keep it light for handling and strong at the same time so it can take the wear and tear. One way to do that is by building things in the 'tapered' style. If we do a flat twenty-four feet high by seven feet wide, it will measure one and three-eighths

Hollow arm of Act 3
throne

37

Old Vic Annexe w
Act 3 window

inches at the bottom and fifteen–sixteenths of an inch at the top. That tapering removes weight without altering strength or function. You can also leave out the inside of things–we only make what will be seen. We build the entire upstage arm of a throne because the audience is looking upstage and some of them will be able to see it. But all we build of the downstage arm is its downstage face. The side that faces the back of the stage is always invisible to the audience and it serves no function, therefore it doesn't have to be there at all.

"I never know the proposed budget," he continues. "I price a show according to a) how long it will take to build, b) how much material it will need and the price of the material, c) breaking it down and fitting it up, and d) the cost of labour." "There are various ways you can cheat on your costs," Frank chimes in. "For instance, if you have a heavily moulded set, the parts that are going to be seen from the front can be painted rather than built. Straight or square flats are cheaper to build than, say, the Act 3 window flat or a curved flat."

They also figure what basic shapes to build and what to attach or "plant on" in the form of wooden or rubber mouldings, dowels, trim of all kinds. And Tom decides how the pieces of the set will be broken down for touring into small working units. "If you make a chair," says Frank, "it's solid, all one piece. If you build a throne, you can make it as many pieces as it need be, and then reassemble it. You take it down as small as you can, but you can't have thousands of bits or they'd never get it put together."

Tom refuses to be sidetracked: "Then they take my estimate with that of the other departments and see if the total is near what's allocated. If it's too much, then the designer will try to cut down. He can make changes to bring the price down, like making two tops for one platform—rostrum, we call it—instead of building two entire pieces, which saves both labour and materials. So we go back and forth—my estimate to the designer, his changes back to me for another estimate—and when my figures are approved, *then* I start making constructional drawings, only when I know exactly what we're going to build."

"We're about six weeks along on the pillars," Frank concludes, as Tom leaves for his sixty-five-mile journey home. "And there are fourteen pieces with leaves all over them that'll set in for Act 2 and 4. They're all about sixteen feet high. They'll be built here, just timber and canvas. The artist can mark them out and we'll cut them and cover them. We haven't got those flats drawn up yet. Everything gets canvassed before it goes out to be painted, so the colour and texture of the paint on it will be uniform. To keep the weight down, linen or muslin can replace canvas as the covering. Offstage stuff, like platforms and stairs, get felt and canvas covering but no paint. Without the covering, they 'drum'. There's not much meat on the ballet, but you can still hear them offstage."

He relights his pipe. "Get it done as quickly as you can, make a decent job of it, and get it right—that's what I work for, not the whys and wherefores. We take them as they come. A lot of people don't know what they want 'til it's built, and a lot of what they do want is impossible to do. One designer wanted something suspended over the stage. He had it held up on the model with a bit of thread or wire, but he told us he didn't want us to use anything like that that could be seen. So we said to him, 'You do it. When you can get it to stay up on the model without any support, we'll get it to stay up on the stage.'"

11 October. Seven weeks to opening night. Louise Champion, Kim Baker's assistant, is dictating a shopping list to Nicola Parkes in the stockroom: "A/B sequins . . ." that means irridescent ones lacquered with a mother-of-pearl finish, ". . . thousands and thousands of them. For all the swan bodices." "Flat or cup?" Nicola asks. Even sequins call for decisions. "Some and some, and a quarter of an inch across. And quite small ordinary pearls, not quite microscopic. And drop pearls as well, masses of them . . ." A mass is twelve strands, about 250 pearls in all, and they're starting to buy them in cartons of several thousand.

Nicola and her assistant Linda deal daily with the tiniest tangible bits of the costumes—cases of pearls, strings of sequins—and the strongest bits—calico and cotton lining fabrics—and everything that connects them or decorates them. Their stockroom, just down the hall from the Pattern Room, spills over onto several other floors, into many locked cupboards, and even into a warehouse near the Strand and storage space in Kent. "Obviously," says Nicola, "if we kept *everything* in stock, we'd be the whole Opera House. We just had about £9000 worth of tights delivered and we don't know where to put them." They command a treasure trove of materials, many of which they describe as "hard . . . no, impossible to find any more. If a place is closing down or if a manufacturer stops making something, they let us know and we buy the ends of it, just so we have it." Special Cupboard No. 3 is packed with these treasures: jet beads, chenille fringe, tassels, leather gloves, odd-shaped silver sequins, belt buckles, fans.

The wardrobe offices bulge with pattern sheets, which document every costume by listing the source, price and yardage–with swatches–of every fabric in it. A whole room bulges with rolls and bolts of leftover fabric, each marked with the production's title and date and often the character's name as well. Everything–well, nearly everything–can be remade from stock.

Like the delectable sweets waiting on trays in a confectioner's window, the contents of the stockroom defy description. The available variety, and the sheer quantities, reduce you to making lists: All different weights and textures of net; cotton net, "bra net" which doesn't rip, DN-1–the stiffest net made and only one mill in England still makes it– for tutus. Lace, delicate as spiderwebs or clotted with cotton knots. A ribbon cupboard. A braid cupboard. On the shelf, twenty-five boxes of white cotton thread, ten rolls to the box, 1000 metres to the roll. Boxes of shoelaces, of snap fasteners, of hooks and bars arranged by size in both black and silver and marked 'tutu,' 'corset,' 'trousers and skirts.' Boxes of

Fabric in stockroom

40

buttons marked Military, Metal, Covered, White, Plastic, Diamante, Fancy. Boxes of elastic: pink, white, black. Stiff collars. Scraps of fur. Tins of jewels.

★   ★   ★

Five floors below in the music library, paper, India ink, and a photocopy machine represent the only essential supplies. Day after day, four people labour in this one room like monks toiling over their beloved manuscripts.

The original, complete score of *Swan Lake*, bound in a thick, blue book, runs 685 pages. When the ballet was first done by the Royal Ballet, selections from that volume were hand-copied in India ink onto negative, clear paper which lasts forever. Each negative was then photographed, and the parts for each instrument printed from the photographs. "As long as you want to use the same music," says assistant librarian Gina Boaks, "you keep printing from the same negative. But when you decide to do something different with the music, you must either copy it out again the way you want it, transpose what you've got, or insert the bits that are missing. For every instrument, of course." Gina is six months pregnant and has a terrible cold, but her voice gathers speed and enthusiasm as she starts turning pages.

"The only way to explain what happens is to look at one specific number. Here's No. 17 in the original score; it's the first selection in Act 3, a fanfare and waltz repeated three times called *La Sortie des Invités et la Valse*. It will be No. 21 in the score we're preparing now." Each of these numbers–this one is twenty-three pages long in the full score–is broken down by rehearsal figures of roughly thirty-two bars each, which are the same in all scores and parts. They're the only fixed reference point the musicians have got. If the conductor asks them all to play at "two bars before Fig. 12," everyone will refer to exactly the same place.

According to Gina, No. 17 breaks down like this in the bound score:
Rehearsal Figures
13–14 = fanfare and short passage in 6/8 time
14–15 = waltz
15–16 = fanfare and short passage in 6/8, identical to 13–14, no change of key
16–17 = waltz, basically the same tune but with bigger orchestration
17–18 = identical fanfare
18–19 = identical to 14–15 waltz
19–20 = repeat 16–17 waltz
20–21 = 14–15 waltz with slightly different orchestration
21–23 = a brand-new middle section of the waltz, whole new musical idea
23–24 = same as 20–21
24–25 = same as 16–17
25–end = same as 14–15, ending with repeated cadences to finish things off neatly.

"In the '79 version, the last time changes were made, you started with the fan-fare, Figure 13 to 14, and then missed everything out 'til Fig. 18. Played 18 to 22, cut 22 to 23, played 24 to 25 but without the repeat that is in the original. Then you cut sixteen bars of Fig. 25, played the next twenty-four bars, cut six bars and played the last three bars.

"For this version, they'll play 13 to 18 in full, cut to Fig. 25 and play forty bars of it, cut the next six bars and play the last three. That's shorter than the original, but longer than the '79 version.

"Another problem for us is that you have to copy so the turn-over of the page is right for the musician playing it. Parts must be specially written out for this reason. Even-numbered pages are always on the left; those pages don't need turning over. But odd-numbered pages must be worked out so that at the bottom of the page, where the musician will have to turn it, there is a space in the music, either bars of rest or the end of the piece. A short right page followed by a long left one won't work. What you do is print the short bit of music on the left page, give the facing right-hand page a number so the printer will know it *is* a page, a blank one, and then start the next long piece on the left.

"We heard in the spring that a new *Lac* was coming, but we didn't get any details 'til mid-May. Then the first two acts were done, printed roughly by the end of August, and then the order of the numbers was changed, so we had to re-ink numbers on the individual pieces and rearrange the sequence before they were bound. We got the details of Act 3 and 4 the beginning of September, and final information on them during the last week of September. One of the variations and the coda for the Act 3 Princesses' dance are completely new; they're from the Appendix of the original Russian score. And Numbers 27 and 28 have never been done here before, so *all* the orchestration, every orchestral part, needs writing out. And Number 29 needed transposing to fit with the other changes around it. We had a transposed version in the negatives, but it was a cut version and Peter wanted it done in full."

At the moment, the photocopier is broken, Tom is away on holiday, and Louise is temporarily deaf on one ear. Richard and Gina are fine.

So are Jennifer Adey and her two assistants, Bridget and Lesley, in the millinery department on the top floor. "We were due to start *Lac* two weeks ago," Jennie explains, with her habitual bright grin, "but then all three of us were ill, so we only started last Tuesday.

"Now, three or four people may wear the same costume, but it doesn't always follow for heads. The body size is not relevant to the head size. When the dancers first enter the company, we take a complete set of standard measurements. The important ones are 1) the round, taken over the fullest part of the head, around the brow, 2) ear to ear, taken over the top, and 3) brow to nape. The ballet girls seem to have very small heads; the smallest girl is twenty and a half inches around and the largest only twenty-three inches.

"Anything that goes on the head and the hat is done here – beadwork, tassels . . . –everything except feathers which we buy curled and dyed to specification. Generally, if it's purely wire and plonks on the head it's a headdress. If it's wire and fabric and more heavily machined, it comes to me. There's no hard and fast distinction."

So far they've made the prototype, the model-for-approval-by-the-designer, of the Neapolitan boys' hats, a shallow crown with a brim that curls up in the back and swoops down more gently into a long point in the front. "Some designers will approve the prototype, some want to see it on the boy. You need to see it with a body *and* the costume. I mean, if you've got frocks with great big sleeves, you've got to proportion the hats to those. Once the prototype is approved, the hats just flow off the assembly line here. We usually make the basic number plus one." She has blocked the Neapolitan boys' crown on a form and cut the brim from a paper pattern. Both are made out of espartra, which is the trade name for sheets of light woven straw with linen glued to one side. Once it's dampened, it can be shaped, stretched, moulded and wired. Jennie says the millinery motto is 'When in doubt, cut it on the cross,' across the material you're using because you always need the flexibility of fabrics.

"The ways you make hats to go into shops and to go on the stage are as different as chalk and cheese. We use two layers of everthing *and* Rigilene–that's flexible boning that stops the hats from crushing–and wiring. We've given up using millinery wire because it's not strong enough. We now use piano wire. The stuff we make now will still be going strong at the turn of the century." Like all the costumes, the hats will be in and out of wicker packing cases called skips

LEFT Jennifer Adey making a Spanish hat
RIGHT Prototype for Neapolitan boys' hats

throughout the long tour. By building the hats to last now, Jennie is saving time and energy for herself and money for the management for the next twenty years.

In the Pattern Room, Louise is only worrying about the present. "We'll be hustling right up to the last minute. We're running out of suppliers of black fabric in all of London. And we can't get any more of that gold net either, that all the waltz girl skirts are made of." Her shopping list now includes dotted net, black veiling, gold net, A/B sequins, pearls. And black taffeta to line the Queen Mother's velvet skirt: "A real taffeta, like a '50s ballgown taffeta," says Susanna. "*Stiff,* like *tin,*" says Philip. "I'm sorry about the velvet. Of course it *looks* wonderful, but I don't want drippy Grecian folds but stiff blocks of folds." Hence the additional lining.

Nesta Brown, who is about to order the shoes, waits patiently in the doorway to consult with Philip. He answers her before she asks anything, picking up where he left off the last time they spoke: "For the pages, a boot with a one and a half inch heel, black suede, straight-sided, not shaped or fitted. It doesn't have to be a ballet boot. And for Rothbart, a ballet boot but with a heel." "You can't have a ballet boot with a one and a half inch heel," Nesta puts in. Philip goes on, ". . . Rothbart should be fitted up the leg, high calf, and cut straight across."

"How do you fit the pages when they're all extras?"

"Everyone's a size nine anyway, aren't they? Get them larger rather than smaller and they can wad them out, wear extra thick socks and things."

All the workrooms are now busy and each of them adds a few pieces to the complex wardrobe puzzle. Gordon Hutchings, grey-haired, blue-eyed and plump around the middle though he was once a dancer, is marking out braid patterns on the boys' tunics for the *pas de six* in Act 3. He says with some dismay, "Philip did a very delicate bit of drawing that's going to get a very wide braid. And he wants straight braid put around circles; you'll have to pleat it up like a rosette to get it to fit. I went up to get the braids from Louise, and they're not even ordered yet. I'm ready to put them on. The trouble is, I've got to trace this pattern on all the other tunics, and none of them are the same size." Identical costumes are not carbon copies of each other. Since the dancers are different widths across the chest, different lengths from shoulder to waist or hip, the proportions of the design, the relation of one braid to another and of both of them to the body, must be worked out anew for each dancer. "It helps a lot if you know the boy and can picture the body. I like to take my own measurements; you can have twenty boys exactly the same measurements and entirely different shapes." He has six people to hand things to, but he does all the cutting himself. "I haven't sorted out the Act 1 waltz boys yet. Their tunics are basically stripes on a black background, folded up against their chests and held with a belt. You have about six fabrics, six colours, to make stripes out of. It's still not worked out."

Audrey Ward and her seven girls are making the Act 1 waltz girls and nothing else, except ten *Alceste* costumes. There are four waltz girls, but they're making ten costumes: "I'd like to have them all done, all ten, for the first dress rehearsal.

Braid patterns

I believe in getting all the casts done. You never know. For *Beauty*, here at the Opera House, we had five casts for Bluebird and we thought we'd do the first three. But I went ahead and made all five, and by the first night they'd juggled about so much that the fifth of those five Bluebirds went on." Fonteyn, Somes, Sibley, Mason, Beriosova, Nerina, Blair and MacLeary leap and pose in black and white over her cutting table, and a red bullseye beside Sir Frederick Ashton proclaims him 'Supreme Choice.' Twenty-six years at the Opera House endow Audrey with equanimity. "I don't feel pressed for time. We're fitting the week of the 26th and if nothing is drastically changed, we'll be all right for time. You never work from start to finish, straight along. Once it's ready for fitting, you leave it and go on to something else."

Gordon was padding the bodices for the Neapolitan girls. "They're the tinies," he said, "Ann Carol and Sandra. Philip wants the bodices to sit one and a half inches away from their chests." Now Audrey is padding the waltz girls' hips, around the side and back but not over the stomach. She will handstitch the wrap-around pad into the costume so it can be removed for washing. "Philip wants one more thickness on what I've already made."

At the other end of the same huge room, Sue Dempster completes Audrey's thought. "We must get it to look as he want it to," she says firmly. "How we do it is up to us." She and her five workers are building the Act 3 *pas de six* girls' costumes, brilliantly red and gold. The arithmetic of their work is exactly like Audrey's. There are three girls in the *pas de six* and nine costumes in preparation:

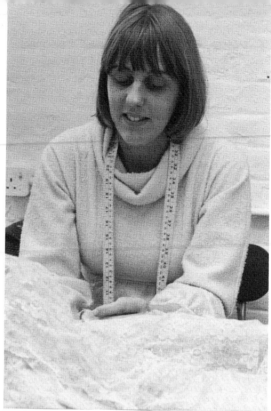

ABOVE LEFT Audrey Ward

ABOVE Susan Dempster

LEFT Fitting the Neapolitan costume: (left to right) Gordon Hutchings, Ann Carol, Louise Champion

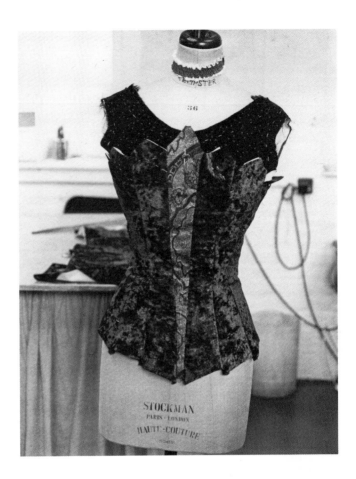

"Flower petal" bodice for
Act 3 *pas de six*

all of the first and second casts, one of the third and one of the fourth, "and we just got the ninth name on Monday. We've had the designs about three weeks.

"We're in between now. We've got work to do, but we haven't got the material to carry on with." It is a lavish design, incorporating seven different fabrics. The bodice looks like flower petals stitched together vertically so the shoulders and head will blossom above them, and the black and gold lace topskirt, with its long free-floating panels, will flare dramatically below them. All the petals but the largest, centre one will be red velvet; except for a central strip, the panels will be entirely tomato brocade. One fabric, a black and gold brocade, will fill both those key positions, and *that* fabric is what Sue is waiting for. "But we can't make the topskirt anyway, even if we had the black and gold, because we haven't yet got the net for the underskirts. Maybe it's being dyed, maybe it's being pleated, I don't know. We've got the sleeve material, but we can't do those without the rest of the bodice. And we're held up on *Alceste* too."

Nesta Brown doesn't have to wait for materials–she has to go out and secure them herself. Along with maintaining and keeping track of the shoes in the active repertory of the Royal Ballet, tasks lumped together under the heading of "running wardrobe," she also has sole charge of "production wardrobe"—the ordering and detailed instructions concerning the making of new shoes—for both that company and the Sadler's Wells Royal Ballet.

"I always feel it's like a campaign more or less. First I get a cast list. Then I have an interview with the designer. Only one of Philip's drawings has a shoe in it, and I have to discuss the details even if there have been feet in the drawings. Then, with *Swan Lake*, they wanted prices. I describe what I want to the shoemakers and they do a working drawing, which translates the artist's conception to something practical, something technically possible, that the pattern can be cut from. The price is based on the amount of work and the amount of leather used: the higher the boot, the higher the price. In the meantime, we have masses of cast changes, and I go through the list to see where shoes can double. One pair of boots will do for the same dancer when he's Benno and again when he's just a boy in the corps. Then after the OK is given on the estimate, I make out the actual order.

"There is only one shoemaker for character shoes, Anello and Davide, the only ones in the world I think. A character shoe is anything that's not a ballet slipper or a pointe shoe. Philip looked at the catalogue of what they ordinarily make and told me the adjustments he wanted in their basic shapes. Then I order the shape in the catalogue and specify the designer's modifications. You must keep in mind too the colours they stock and the quantities they have of those colours. If they only have enough of one colour leather to make nine pair of boots but you need twelve, you *don't* use it, because you could never dye it to match exactly. You can't dye suede—it goes horrible.

"Before I turn the order in, I have to check all the sizes. I have drawings of all their feet and measurements right up to the knees, because the shoemaker doesn't see these dancers. I keep a file, but I had measurements taken again for *Swan Lake* because I wanted it to be exact.

"Then I collect the shoes from Anello, and make sure they're not too high or the wrong colour or with the wrong heels on. Especially with *Swan Lake*, one tries to have the shoes so there's time to make corrections. But you don't want to get them to the company too soon, or they'll put them on and wear them down right away.

"It's essential to know the girls, to know what they will and won't wear or can't wear. I've had this job eight or nine years. The designer doesn't know their bunions or their injuries. If they've had operations on their Achilles, it leaves scar tissue and you have to watch that in boots. I can say to a designer, 'That girl isn't steady on that heel. It's not safe for her.' It's like translating, all the time, putting on ballets."

Tom Walker, at the Old Vic Annexe, says it another way: "None of it is extremely difficult. You don't need academic degrees. You need a bit of experience, and a bit of common sense to apply it." They lost a week on *Lac* because

Designer's model for
Act 1 towers

they had to work on *Sonnambula*, but now they've finished the two Act 1 towers, which differ slightly from the other six columns, and put them on castors "because they have to disappear." The three windows–*three* windows?–for Act 3 are also finished, right down to the trim of paper rope and both wooden and rubber moulding. "It's always best to work under pressure," he admits.

But "you virtually have to be clairvoyant," says Mike, never letting go of his long-handled brush down at the London Opera Centre. Robin is out with a cold; Mike and Dave carry on calmly without him. "Until the designer came last week," Mike says, "we didn't know what else we'd be painting. Now we find we've got two more windows, pillars, and a backcloth of clouds and sea that we started today. We haven't got room to spread it out 'til this orange one's approved."

They had planned originally to spray all the muslin orange and paint it to darken it. "We were going to spray the canvas with black dye and stick the

49

London Opera
Centre: Robin Snow
with Act 2 branches

orange muslin down over it. But Philip wanted the top material black, not orange, so you got the darkness in the folds. If you look at the painting of this backcloth in the model, there are areas that are more black, more gold, more orange. Those are reproduced as closely as possible; so are the folds of the ruching in the muslin. You must interpret the model exactly, even those areas that might have been accidental or random. You go up the ladder with the diminishing glass to see how close you've come. It's much harder than painting something very realistic, because the designer relies on how you interpret it. You could either make this detail look interesting or just a mess."

Philip has also examined the tangle of branches for Act 2–officially deemed a border because they frame the stage but do not touch it–and decided they are not "high" enough, textured enough. They have been assembled like a sandwich: drop cloth cut into branches first, a layer of strawberry netting laid over the cutout to fix the branches in position and keep them from flopping onto each other, and black fabric called casement cloth or bolting ruched up along each branch for the raised texture. To add height, Dave is now gluing snakey strips of foam rubber to the crumpled bolting and covering them with still more of it. "You slap glue on the back of it, put it down in place over the foam strips, and slap a bit more glue on top to make sure the fabric is completely glued and you don't have to go back later and make the job a little longer by touching up the spots where

50

it's coming loose." Dave passes the entire afternoon this way, taking great pains over a mundane, repetitive task. Perhaps knowing that he will never have to do it again—for this production anyway—eases his boredom.

★   ★   ★

The headdress and jewelry department, on the top floor of 45 Floral Street, is a magpie's attic that would fit easily into one corner of the vast draughty paint shop. There is not a bare surface anywhere. Leonardo and Botticelli, Fonteyn and Princess Margaret, photos and postcards paper the walls. The shelves over-flow with books, lengths of chain, tins of beads, *diamanté*, ribbon. The work-tables are loosely packed nests of wire and pliers and clots of beeswax, tiny jars of paint with even tinier brushes, glue and tissues. Chocolate boxes might hold chocolate almonds or jet beading.

Jean Percival and her two assistants, Alison and Jackie, revel in the clutter. "I haven't gone near *Swan Lake* since that fitting at the Wells," Jean says. "We've been on other things all this time. We're doing twenty-five swan headdresses and eight for the principals—that's Odette and Odile for each of the four—and that is all, I'm afraid. None of the jewelry because we're doing *Alceste* as well.

Texturing the Act 2
borders

51

We started *Lac* around the time of the fitting at the Wells, and were doing *Samson* all September at the same time. It's very difficult switching from ethnic African jewelry to *Swan Lake*.

"People think things for the stage have to be so much bigger than life, but the dancers aren't bigger than life. You have to make things in scale for the dancers and the bodies, not for the stage itself. I very often do my own drawings, just to see what I'm going to do and how. Sometimes the designer's drawings are not even very human. It's equally trying if they give you specific measurements, because you'll start to make it and it won't actually fit. It's eye more than any-thing—you can't measure.

"The problem with the *Swan Lake* principals is that all the sizes and shapes are different. This one's Samsova, who's got rather a wider face, whereas Marion Tait's is quite tiny. You don't just repeat the design; it's basically the same, but with minute variations. If you got all the Odettes together and took a picture of them all, you'd see that every one is slightly different.

"The rest of the swans won't be different except for the head sizes. Fortunately, dancers are all a pretty standard size. We never get a chance to fit them . . . well, there's nothing to fit until they're made. You can't actually pin the work on their heads for a proper fit. We're good at guessing. That fitting at the Wells was the first time I ever tried a headdress on before they were all made. And I made that one in the middle of *Samson* because I wanted to be sure Peter Wright liked it before I made twenty-five.

"We ordered everything for this. The mesh comes from France. They've stopped making it now too, so we'll not get any more. That happens all the time. We're dependent on fashion; if evening dresses haven't got any beading on them, the suppliers stop importing it and then we can't get any. Anyway, the mesh came in gold and bright blue, so it had to be dyed in the paintshop downstairs. It's like the gold mesh you see in bags of sweets hanging on Christmas trees. There's about two and a half metres of it in each headdress, and the equivalent of about three headdresses work in each swan: the frame, the covering on it–that's the mesh and feathers and trim–and the tiara thing and its decoration . . . which is why we're doing *only* swans.

"The frame is millinery wire but of inferior quality. Good stuff you bend and it holds its shapes, but the supply of *that* has dried up. This stuff doesn't hold anything–it bends on its own. The milliners use piano wire but that hardly moves or bends at all, and you couldn't possibly get it into all these twiddly shapes for decoration. They're made of crin, which is metallic cord made in Switzerland. Suchard's ties up its chocolate boxes with it. The thinner cord comes on a roll with a very thin wire inside it; the heavier cord we have to thread with wire ourselves. There's 100 metres in a roll of this thin sort that I'm using for the twiddles, and we've used a couple of rolls already. Whenever you've got a moment to spare, you just sit twiddling the wire into shape to make twenty-five of those swans.

"The mesh will cover the frame; then we'll put white felt, cut roughly in the shape of feathers, on top of that and then white feathers. The felt is there to attach the feathers to and to hold them in the proper shape. Then the pearls that frame the face are sewn to the mesh. But the pearls in the tiara are wired on, not sewn. The new crin is more fragile than the old stuff and it just unravels when you stitch on it.

"The dancers do terrible things in the headdresses: lay their head against someone's face for example. Or do their hair, put on their headdress, and then spray over the whole thing with hair lacquer–I've seen them do that. Then someone complains that the stones aren't as shiny as they should be or that the whole headdress is looking rather tatty. And these won't last long, I don't imagine. They used to hold up for twenty-five years, but I don't see how these can. And it's a shame; just as much work goes into making it out of poor quality materials as out of good ones."

*   *   *

Incredibly, there is one last workroom involved with *Swan Lake* on the top floor. Edward Percival (no relation to Jean) is making the extremely ornate dresses for the three women in the Act 3 Czardas. "I'm making eight frocks, but the lead frock is different from the side girls, which cuts down the number of ways you can swap them around. So I'm making two leads and six side girls. I wanted to work on *Swan Lake* but I didn't think I'd have time, and then these

Edward Percival

were left over to be done so I'm doing them. I'm starting late because I've got frocks to do for *Alceste* and for Mme. Cotrubas for *Sonnambula*."

He gestures wearily at the black velvet, gold lamé, and gold, orange and muted red–black brocades that billow over his cutting table. "There's the last of my fabric, still wet from the dying. By the time you've got all the gold braid on and the ribbon in between, you won't be able to see what's under it anyway so it doesn't matter what colour it is. Gold braid is hard on the eyes, bad for your scissors–it blunts them–and if you sew on 200 metres of it, your fingers will start to fray at the ends." He rolls his eyes comically, and returns to his preparations for Mme. Cotrubas. *Lac* will have to wait.

19 October. Six weeks to opening night. Bulletins from the wardrobe: Sue Dempster's black and gold topskirt fabric finally arrived. She has cut it, backed it with a layer of net, and sent it out again to be pleated. She's also received her black and gold brocade, so the two halves of the red velvet bodice are joined at last. But she still can't cut the loose panels for the skirt because she doesn't know what size to cut them. The entire skirt will be fuller with the pleated topskirt on it than it is now, and the panels must be in proportion to the overall shape.

Audrey Ward is replacing a slice of lacey black fabric on the shoulders of the Act 1 waltz dresses with a slice of rusty-gold instead. Philip has decided he'd

54

made a mistake choosing the first of them. At least she has enough of the second.

Jennie Adey reports that Philip wants the Neapolitan boys' hats to have straight rather than curved sides on the brim, and a more rounded point that droops further in the front. Once he approves the changes, they'll cover the entire espartra shape in soft cotton batting called icewool to keep the straw weave from showing, and then cover the batting with black jersey. And the hats still won't be finished; there are feathers and a beaded silk scarf yet to be made and attached.

Gordon Hutchings is in between: "I've got to stop to wait for the braid. I haven't done the girls at all. I'd rather get all the boys set first." The Neapolitan girls' underskirts, clouds of black tulle, hang side by side from a pipe on the ceiling.

26 October. Five weeks to opening night. The company has returned from Yugoslavia and gone back into rehearsal at Sadler's Wells. In two weeks, they will pack their bags and leave town again, for a week in Oxford, a week in Newcastle, and a week in Manchester where Thursday night has been reserved for one final dress rehearsal the night before *Lac* opens to the public and the critics.

In the Cranko Room at the top of the Wells, they are tackling Act 4 again. Both Jennie Mills and Siobhan Stanley are now off, and June Highwood has replaced Siobhan as the Big Swan opposite Mandy-Jayne Richardson. There are at

Big Swans. (left to right) June Highwood and Mandy-Jayne Richardson

least four students in the room who are here, Debbie Chapman says bleakly, "to learn it." But as they begin work, there is a gaping hole in the swans' formation: Dido Nicholson is at a fitting. Someone will now always be at a fitting.

They dance the first ensemble and then cut at once to the end of the *pas de deux*. Without the principals, Peter can't block the entire act, map out the details of who moves where when. But the principals don't expect to dance, not this early in the game anyway. They can dance in their own rehearsals.

Although Peter has seated the swans for the *pas de deux*, scattering them around the stage like snowdrifts, he hasn't told them when to stand up. Counting "an 8 and a 6 and a slow 1 and 2 and 3," backward from the end of the *pas de deux*, he chooses that 3 for their cue. Once they're up, they can move into new positions, but "on the trill after the *pirouette*" this time rather than on a count. Sometimes the counts control them, sometimes the mood or flow of the music. They may be asked to follow either–or a change of lights or the turn of a head, or anything at all–and must be prepared to do it, remember it, reproduce it.

Having set that much of Act 4, to the end of the *pas de deux*, Peter announces, "We're going to do basically the Sergeyev version, with a few tiny changes." Most of the corps is too young to know that he's talking about the original Royal Ballet version, but they don't have to know it either. They are told to hold their present position and then count two 8s, a 6, then three 8s and a 10, then go into a big backbend with arms opening. Hold that for an 8 and then arms up and turn. Peter is staging Rothbart's dramatic appearance and his attempts to separate Odette and Siegfried, but for now, the drama of the scene must take second place to its organization.

Staging Act 4. Peter Wright, Alain Dubreuil and corps de ballet

In rehearsal: (left to right) Peter Wright, Debbie Chapman, Desmond Kelly

Act 2. Corps de ballet

ABOVE At the piano:
Barry Wordsworth and
Hilary Bell

LEFT Corps de ballet

The swans circle the stage in alarm before funnelling their panicked flight into two parallel lines that form a long diagonal alley pointing to the down right corner of the stage. To keep Odette away from Rothbart, Siegfried flips her up onto his shoulder in "the Bluebird," the same position in which the Bluebird in *Sleeping Beauty* carries Princess Florine, and bears her out of reach. "Can you change the lift?" Peter calls out over the hubbub, hoping that two things will happen. First he wants David Ashmole to execute a *pressage*, that is, to press Galina straight up over his head from her perch on his shoulder so she floats above the fray. And that's not all—next he wants Alain Dubreuil, Rothbart, to pluck her out of David's hands, lift her right off David's fully extended arms. When he asks for the *pressage*, Galina, David and Alain reply together, "No way!"

So Peter leaves them to solve it by themselves and turns his attention to the diagonal: "Go back to where you start the run. We've got to get the heights right whatever we do. Which of you is usually the smallest?" While they run, the swans will have to shift places, slot into a different order, so that when they stop in their two lines the heights descend evenly from June and Mandy-Jayne. They must also leave enough room in the alley for Odette, borne aloft by Rothbart, to soar down its length. "Galina, you have to be down the diagonal at the end of

Alain Dubreuil carries
Galina Samsova as
David Ashmole
watches

59

"We've got to get the heights right." Peter Wright and corps de ballet

three 8s." "I'm easy," she laughs, "I'm being carried."

The swans in the diagonal now whirl about and lunge toward the lake. "When she jumps, you go into that long lunge. That's your position for Odette's death." And after her death, the triangular wedge of swans that has separated Siegfried and Rothbart must be repositioned to become an oblong phalanx headed by the Big Swans. Again the sizes have to be graded, and every flap of a wing assigned a count.

They face a solid month of these moment by moment changes and choices, the girls rather more than the boys. "There's not much for me in *Lac*," one of the boys admits without a hint of disappointment in his voice, "just the odd Czardas–that's about three minutes–or the Polacca in Act 1–that's another two minutes . . . five minutes dancing for me. But I don't mind really. I'm very busy in *Fille* and *Shrew*, and I don't really want to do all that 'ballet' dancing. They're all going spare about getting this thing on, but it'll get on OK–it always does–and once it's open everything'll settle down."

The girls see it differently. Nibbling her cheese and salad at lunch, one of them explores what's coming a little more explicitly: "Everyone's very excited about this *Swan Lake*. I can't wait to see all the bits put together and the costumes and all. I've seen the things *I'll* wear and they're very beautiful. But the waltz one for Act 1 . . . The dance is very hard, lots of difficult partnering. It's hard enough to do it in just leotards and these flimsy rehearsal skirts, but the dresses have those tight fitted sleeves and bodices. I'll want my hooks out half an inch anyway, otherwise I'll feel I won't be able to breathe enough to get through it.

"And he's also padded a lot of the dresses. Well, I know the look he's trying to get, with the round busts and hips and the tiny waists . . . But we spend so much time watching our weight, and it's so helpful if you can look at yourself before you go on and like what you see. We're all basically straight in shape in this company; our busts, waists and hips are very nearly the same size. So if you pad our busts and hips, the indented waist looks ridiculous, so to keep it in proportion you widen that as well–and then we're *still* straight, but wider."

The first cast of the Spanish divertissement–Alain, Carl Myers, Sami Saidi, and June–have been at fittings too, and when Carl says, "I've got pants out to here, giant jodphurs. I'll be miles away from you, Sami," it's not just idle chat. They must adjust to the costumes as they do to the steps, so both look totally natural on them.

They dance without a hitch. Their lips move as they count, but no one stumbles even once. Galina corrects only details, hands and *épaulement*. Then suddenly, each of the four is teaching the dance to his counterpart in the second cast: Carl with Stephen Wicks, Alain with Nick Millington, June with Chenca Williams, Sami with Mandy-Jayne. Without music, each duo proceeds at its

Spanish Dance. Carl Myers, Samira Saidi, Alain Dubreuil, June Highwood

Marion Tait and Pe[ ]
Wright

The three Princesses
(left to right) Petal
Miller, Margaret
Barbieri, Sherilyn
Kennedy

own pace. The room gets very noisy, but no one's concentration wavers even slightly. Stephen has pulled a groin muscle and is officially off, but he marks the dance in his street clothes and seems to know it almost on sight. After an hour, Alain jokes, "And that's the good news. The bad news is that we've got castanets to play at the same time."

The next day, Marion Tait arrives at the theatre for the first time all season. She is leaning on a cane and a blue plastic bag envelops her right foot, from which a nerve has been removed. Although originally one of the first four Odettes, no one has yet said when she will actually dance the role. But if she can walk she can come in and watch, and once she is watching, she is learning.

They have two hours immediately after class to run through Act 3, which staggers forward spasmodically while Peter directs traffic. Czardas goes smoothly until the very end, when all three couples stop at the same instant saying, "Two beats too many." At least two extra casts, marking, shadow both Sherilyn Kennedy as the Hungarian Princess and Margaret Barbieri as the Polish

Act 2. Galina Samsova and David Ashmole

Princess. Mazurka is still very ragged; the distinction is seldom clear between the hiccuping skip of the mazurka step, the straight 1–2–3 waltz of a *balancé*, and a simple accented run.

Petal Miller's solo for the Italian Princess is set to the music that was used for the Act 3 *pas de deux* in the original Moscow production. What is customarily used today as Black Swan music actually comes from Act 1. Restoring Act 3 music to Act 3 is one of the ways in which Barry Wordsworth has tried to bring musical order to the chaotic tamperings the score has suffered over the years. Peter's three Princesses impose an equally welcome dramatic logic on Act 3. In most productions, the Queen Mother thrusts a bevy of unattached beauties at her son during the ball, and then distracts him from choosing a wife with an entertainment comprising Hungarian, Polish, Neapolitan and Spanish dances. Did you ever wonder who the beauties were or why the entertainers were so singularly international? To answer those questions and tie up the narrative loose ends, Peter has turned the nameless ladies into Princesses, each of whom is escorted to the castle by a grand ambassador and a splendid entourage. Each Princess dances for the Prince; each entourage dances to entertain the court. What could be simpler? Logic blends with tradition when the Spanish dancers enter behind Odile and Rothbart, and are thus seen to be their entourage.

Step by step, Peter next stages Siegfried's rejection of the three Princesses, the fanfare heralding the late arrivals at the reception, and Odile's entrance with Rothbart. They stumble through it once, begin to fit it together the second time, and then, after the Spanish dance, Galina and Alain perform the *pas de deux* full out. Every eye in the room watches Galina, who does nothing to command their

Peter Wright sets Ac 3 mime with (left to right) David Ashmo Desmond Kelly, Ala Dubreuil, Anita Landa

Mazurka: "the wheel"

attention except move and dance, act and react, like a ballerina rather than an ordinary dancer. Her attitude creates an aura that surrounds her like perfume. You can see some of the dancers following its scent with their eyes and hands and tiny unconscious adjustments of posture, as if trying to learn it, isolate its essence.

Peter adds two 8s of definite freeze during the vision. The court's conversations must stop cold and resume, sixteen counts later, or the effect is lost. Next he sets the mime for Siegfried, Rothbart, Odile and the Queen Mother, straight through to the end of the act. But there is a question about the music when Siegfried discovers he has been deceived by Odile and Rothbart, the exposure-of-the-trick music. What Hilary plays sounds wrong to Peter. "We can't set it now if we're not absolutely sure what the music will be," he says. "We'll set it in Oxford."

They use the extra ten minutes for another go at the Mazurka, specifically at the moment when all eight dancers meet in a straight line, facing front and back alternately, with hands meeting and gripping across stomachs and behind backs. They call it "the wheel." Which of them has to turn around on himself to be facing the right direction? Should they all turn the same way?

They break at 2:00 for lunch and reassemble an hour later, in fresh practice clothes, for Act 4. They begin, as always, with 'the storm.' Counting 2,6,6,8,8,8,10 from Rothbart's entrance, Peter rehearses them like mobile statues: one count of 6, then full stop, the next count of 6, full stop, all the way through.

Act 4. Peter Wright and
Bess Dales

The corps sequence that coincides with the Rothbart-Siegfried fight over Odette is five counts of 8 and keeps getting changed. Should their two diagonal lines lean in opposite directions, away from the alley between them, or in the same direction? And which direction is *that*? Lunging onto which leg? Which arm swoops forward? Does it pass beside the body or over the head? Peter says, "You have two 8s to get into those diagonal lines." Anita says, "They're not getting into *arabesque* in time." Peter says, "They'll have to run faster." The girls say nothing; they count, and run faster.

When Galina mimes, "Here I die," the swans are standing still. Peter shakes his head: "No, there has to be something for you there. You wouldn't just blandly watch your queen go by." He lifts them up on pointe, a little *bourrée* like a shiver, as she makes the gesture for "die," and then settles them back on their feet with their arms crooked sorrowfully across their faces.

Then Rothbart has to die and the swans have to be arranged so they are standing up to his power but not upstaging his death scene. Peter only sketches it for now; as always, he has run out of time. "We *must* stop. I'm supposed to finish at 5:00." "You're supposed to finish at half past four," Anita corrects him. "Half past four? Nobody told me." "It's on the callboard," Galina puts in slyly, releasing them all with a laugh. No one but Peter could get away with not reading the callboard.

The calendar demands more and more dancing—continuous dancing, not bits—squeezed into each day's rehearsals. Wednesday's schedule calls for Acts 1 and 2 between noon and 2:00, and Acts 3 and 4 between 3:00 and 5:30. The callsheet reads "Full Call," which means that the entire company will be in the same room. There will be no other rehearsal anywhere. "We always work a

66

week in advance," someone points out, "rehearsing next week's rep this week. And we don't have to rehearse the coming rep, *Fille* and *Shrew*, because we know it so well . . . which is probably why we're doing it. We need the time to rehearse *Swan Lake*."

They run through the Polacca that closes the act first so that Peter can add the two *pas de quartre* girls to the centre section of it, weaving them in and out of the boys like darting bobbins. How fast can it be done? How fast *must* it be done? Once they're gone, he slides Siegfried in among the boys, making him briefly a part of their dance instead of an observer. *Then* they start Act 1. Peter is now providing . . . not quite line readings, but a sort of dramatic context:

"Siegfried should be surprised on his first entrance. 'What's going on here? Why are all these people here?' "

As the first girls come forward to greet him, Desmond mutters, "Dreadful line, girls, for goodness' sake," with real exasperation.

Every time they do the waltz, someone is marking at the end. They need more wind, more stamina, if they're ever going to get through it. Those couples are now clearly Siegfried's friends, and the crossbow is a present, " 'from all of us'," Peter indicates to Nick Millington who hands it to Siegfried, " 'for your birth-day.' It's as if you're saying, 'We really love you.' You're trying to cheer him up. And, Carl, you must thank them." He stages a handshake between Nick and Carl, and then blurts out impatiently, "Once we're on stage, very soon, I'm not

t an early dress
hearsal (note the
bsence of make-up
nd wigs), David
shmole receives the
rossbow from
icholas
Millington

67

During the *pas de quatre:* (left to right) Christine Aitken, David Ashmole, Nicola Katrak

going to have time to say 'Play it like this. Play it like that.' You must play it. That's what these rehearsals are for. I've given you all the steps now–you've got to get into the part."

In the middle of the *pas de quatre*, after Benno and the two girls dance together, six Princes perform Siegfried's solo: Desmond, Alain, Carl, David, Derek Purnell and Stephen Wicks, with Peter, the seventh, on his feet and marking with them in his street clothes. As the pieces come together–the waltz, the two girls, Benno and the Prince–the logic gradually emerges too. Having stated at the start of his scenario that the court is in mourning for the newly-dead king, Siegfried's father, Peter has staged the first act and much of the third in response to that fact. It explains why Siegfried is surprised to find his friends gathered and waiting to dance, and why the Queen Mother is shocked at what appears to be a party. It *is* the Prince's birthday, true enough, but hardly the occasion for a party

Act 1. Desmond Kelly

given his father's recent death. It explains why the girls must coax him into dancing with them, and why his solo, drifting away from them, is so melancholy. All the pieces fit, it all makes sense, which is by no means accidental.

Months later Peter will say, "I've always been unsatisfied with the first act; it's always unbelievable and a bit silly. I've always hated the Queen giving the bow and arrow . . . in public . . . and I've never really understood the peasants. The music wasn't written for peasants. Peasants have been banished out of this corps, and the Queen's not going to have endless flowers pressed on her. And also, Siegfried's young and all that, and I'm sure eighteen-year-olds *did* have tutors, but it just goes against the grain for me.

"I went through lots of stages with the Act 1 music, too. One of the most beautiful things in it for me is the end of the Polacca where everyone goes off and the music changes into the swan music. That's destroyed if you have a solo there for the Prince. Galina said that in Russia, the usual *pas de trois* was a *pas de quatre* for the Prince, Benno and two girls, and that fitted well. *And* it gets the Prince doing something without waiting the whole act to do it. You see, the story of *Swan Lake* is the Prince's story. It must be about him and what's happening to him, and you must keep him busy and involved the whole time."

He restages the end of the act so Nikki Katrak and Christine Aitken wave from the balustrade as the boys go off hunting, and that's it. "Act 2, please. Everyone not in Act 2, thank you very much." Brief and business-like. Act 1 has taken one and a half hours.

Act 2. Corps de ballet

The Queen Mother greeting the Princesses: (left to right) Petal Miller, Margaret Barbieri, Sherilyn Kennedy, Anita Landa

Act 2 proceeds less haltingly. Rothbart appears out of the leaves like an extension of nature, separates Odette and Siegfried, and then brings the swans on and commands them to dance from their midst. There is further logic in that; they are, after all, under his spell. After the ensemble, Peter says, "It will be just as it used to be, with the swans lined up opposite Benno and Siegfried telling him not to shoot. All my ideas of making it logical and reasonable will just have to bow to that."

Sherilyn, today's Odette, is trying to snatch the role out of thin air. Since Peter is concentrating on the corps, she keeps her eyes on Galina, who is miming in the front.

The clock keeps ticking, and by the time they work their way to cygnets, everyone is tired. Peter says, "It's the *pas de chat* that are worst." Nothing is best.

After lunch he sets all the mime that follows the Black Swan *pas de deux* from scraps of paper, with Barry at the piano. This is where they bogged down yesterday. Each Princess is presented to Siegfried in turn, as if the Queen Mother is asking 'Which of these will it be?' Rothbart's mimed conversation with Siegfried about marrying Odile then fills the music until the vision of the weeping Odette appears in the window behind them. Staging this sequence, from the end of Black Swan to the end of Act 3, which is eighty-six bars of music, takes fifty minutes.

The *pas de six*, then the Czardas and Hungarian Princess follow. Peter scolds the Mazurka group: "It hasn't jelled at all yet. It really doesn't look at all nice, rather as if you're all struggling with every step. You *must* practice on your own." The room is very quiet and very still. No one looks at anyone else.

Act 4 falls apart. Sherilyn, Carl and Alain as Rothbart have not had enough rehearsal in it, and only the swans, some of them, know what they're doing. They go through the whole act once, awkwardly, and then start again. Peter changes the *bourrée* he gave them yesterday on Odette's "Here I die," so that they now collapse broken-winged *away* from the lake, as if too distressed to look. Nothing seems fixed from one day to the next. Still, Sherilyn is optimistic: "I quite enjoy *Lac* now, since the beginning of this week really. I still don't think my arms are very good in the white acts, but it's fun now. I love it."

As they clatter back to the dressing rooms, the girls all glance at the callboard. By habit? Searching for a reprieve? The freshest note reads: "To Company from Lili (Sobieralska). I should like to remind all the girls that when you have finished with shoes that have dyed ribbons, please detach them from your shoes and return them to Briar. Ribbon is far too expensive to be thrown away. Thank you."

Thursday. A runthrough from noon to 3:00, with Hilary at the piano, Barry counting, marking his conducting and fixing tempi in his muscles, and Michael Soffe, the deputy stage manager, timing the entire ballet. "If you go over three hours for a performance," he explains, "the orchestra, dancers, wardrobe and stagehands go on overtime. You figure time from curtain time, 7:30–at 10:30 the three hours are up. So your production must fit within those boundaries." After opening night, he reports the actual running time:

Act 1	32 minutes
Pause	4 minutes–"It's normally three, but you figure four to cover yourself. During the change, we've got to get in the columns, the leafy flats, and the staircase, and cover it with the leaf carpet."
Act 2	32 minutes
Interval	15 minutes
Act 3	44 minutes
Interval	15 minutes
Act 4	20 minutes

Total   162 minutes, or two hours and forty-two minutes. No wonder they don't take an interval between Act 1 and 2.

Peter seems to have shifted gears overnight. He is no longer staging: he is directing, right from the start of Act 1. "Benno, make more of your coming on," he urges, and his excitement is contagious, at least this early in the day.

Waltz. "Particularly today for placing, please. Get your patterns right." "Watch your line, girls. Mandy, you're too far forward." "Now to the Prince all the time, aim it to him, yes."

To Hilary and Barry: "At the end of the waltz, they bow, then they bow to the Prince, then they move back, and *then* the music starts."

Benno and the girls: "Now, this is a full runthrough. Play your parts. Perform it. How can I see what's happening to the act?" Nikki misses nearly every double *pirouette*, and finishes her solo practically in tears. Christine is late for the coda section, and when she catches up, Peter snaps, "We changed that, yesterday. What's the point of rehearsing if you don't think about it?" He is harsh but not cruel. They count on him to be harsh, especially when they're tired. If he didn't prod them, they would give up.

Act 2, with Galina, David and Desmond as Rothbart. The room falls quiet everywhere, as if Galina has brought concentration onstage with her. She dances full out in a white practice tutu and a maroon leotard–no marking, no cigarette, no cardigan–and the girls watch her with respect verging on awe.

Swans: "Heads, heads. Remember, no cutey pie!" They form a circle; alternate swans move toward and away from the centre, taking a tiny preparatory step and poising on pointe in *arabesque*, all arms up. "*Arabesque*–hold it!!" and they do, poised on his command. Then he adds, "Soft arms," and they do that

Act 2. Galina
Samsova and David
Ashmole

73

Act 2. Margaret Barbieri
and Desmond Kelly

too. Act 1 has quieted everyone down, shaken out the first sparks, and the swans are together, attentive, controlled.

Three casts dance the *pas de deux*, one behind the other, while Peter patiently picks out individual hands and arms in the corps that are moving at the wrong speed.

Question: When should the corps change feet? When the swans are not actually dancing, they often stand with one leg demurely cocked at the knee behind the other. But they can't stand on the same leg indefinitely or it will stiffen too much to dance on later, so a decision must be made as to when—exactly when, on what single note of the music—they should shift their weight from one foot to the other. They have all relaxed at the sides during the *pas de deux* and cygnets, but Desmond calls, "Swans, stand up," and they get back on two feet to decide.

Before he starts Act 3, Peter manufactures a new exit for the three Princesses and their ambassadors at the end of Black Swan, which he didn't have time to do yesterday. "Don't rush off, Princesses. It's a slow walk off, and on to the next castle." After they've made their stately exit, giggling, Act 3 begins at the beginning and picks up momentum as it goes along.

Czardas. "You'll never be able to do that last turn because your headdresses won't allow it." But having said that, he leaves the turn exactly as it is.

Mazurka. "You all tend to think that because you've got character shoes on you needn't point your feet. But no—it must be very, very elegant, all the way through. It's mostly the girls, but the boys must be careful too. Very elegant."

Neapolitan. "There are two little modifications, but I'll make them later when we have a proper rehearsal." The runthroughs are for something else. The entire company is here; if they stop over every detail, too many people stand around with nothing to do.

Galina tosses off her first solo and asks, laughing, "Can Benno do the *fouettés* for me?" and then does them herself, left hand resting nonchalantly on her hip.

Peter makes all the exits after the *pas de deux* a few bars earlier to clear the stage before Siegfried confronts Rothbart. He then nods to himself, satisfied for the time being, and excuses the boys. The girls put their pointe shoes and tutus back on. There is nothing you could really call a break.

The first swan ensemble in Act 4 stops twice for one of the recently imported, increasingly harried students to figure out which way to turn. Peter reassures her kindly, "It's all right," which only flusters her more.

When Odette and the Prince finally find each other, Peter mutters, "I think there should be a moment of forgiveness. They shouldn't separate quite so fast." He doesn't say it aloud to them, but he says it loud enough that Desmond, who is sitting beside him, can hear it, which is the same as making a note of it. If Peter forgets, there is now one more person who may remember.

From 4:30 to 6:00, Desmond takes a full company rehearsal for *The Taming of the Shrew* in order to put Chenca Williams in as Kate. With Marion and Siobhan Stanley both off, no one remains to dance the leading role except Margaret, who obviously can't do them all. The rehearsal scheduled at the same time for the principals in *Lac* is cancelled. Carl has to be here to partner Chenca, which leaves Sherilyn without her partner. Desmond is conducting this rehearsal, which leaves Margaret without hers. Galina and David did all their work this morning. "I haven't done a call yet," Margaret says. "I've been doing it in the back for weeks and weeks, but there's no point doing that forever. You either have got to do it all or not do it at all. Now we're not doing a full call Saturday as scheduled, just bits and pieces and that's no good."

The next morning, however, is for principals only, Margaret with Desmond and Sherilyn with Carl, with Galina, Alain and Debbie Chapman in charge. They start, logically, with the White Swan *pas de deux*. You can see Desmond throwing Margaret slightly in the lifts, helping her jump higher than she can on her own and heightening the illusion of her attempt to escape. No one will notice; the atmosphere will mask the mechanics. Galina corrects Margaret's hands, wrists and fingers, coaching by examining and questioning the smallest components of every movement. "As soon as you become a swan, the broken wrists come back," she warns, and "You have too many pointing fingers, all over the place." Margaret says later, "Galina says it's too much wrist, but I actually prefer it that way, a little rounded, more decorated. Not that I like my wrists—I'm not saying that—but it's the style I like. When I've seen it, those are the ones I've always liked." Combining her own preference with Galina's suggestions and Peter's requirements, she will come up with her own, individual performance.

Sherilyn is having trouble with the *manège* in Black Swan. When you see it in

Galina Samsova
coaching

the context of Act 3, you see Odile as one continuous whirlwind connecting the four corners of the stage as if boxing Siegfried and the court with enchantment. In fact, the dancer performs two different turns–*piqués* on one foot and *soutenus* on two–and travels for exactly six counts in each direction, starting each six turns at right angles to the last six without slackening speed. Galina says, "Wherever you change to is front. You just have to decide for yourself what distance to cover in each line." Alain suggests, "Do each six in a straight line. Maybe that'll get you around better," better than if she tries to turn the corner by curving her path. Galina again: "The tempo's a little too fast for you, but it's better that way. It pushes you forward instead of letting you relax." Sherilyn pushes forward, without relaxing or speaking or smiling. She does the *manège* again, and then again.

After she's left the studio, Galina comments, "I don't want to break things down too far in rehearsal. That's what you try to do in the classroom instead, about lifting the elbow for a curved arm or stretching the feet. It's too late to do that by the time they come here. Well, I do it anyway, but here in rehearsal they have so many things to remember. Here you have to help them dance."

Saturday, because Peter is out of town, they rehearse only bits in place of the scheduled runthrough, starting with the first and second casts of the *pas de quatre* in Act 1. The second cast has hardly had a step of rehearsal so far. With a grin, Desmond calls their first try "the St. Valentine's Day massacre."

LEFT Act 2. Margaret Barbieri and Desmond Kelly

77

Chenca is stitching ribbons on her pointe shoes. "I'm in Act 1 waltz, and then I don't know what's happening with me in Big Swans. It started out Siobhan and me. Then June came in for Siobhan, but she was too tall for me so they put Mandy in for me. It's that now, but I don't know what happens when Jennie comes back on."

The boys are sitting against the wall under the barre, feet stuck straight out before them, reading, sleeping, waiting. "*Lac*'s kind of a drag today. I mean, I know the bits need the work, but you give your all at the full calls, when Peter's there, so these little bits just feel like something stuck in to keep us busy while he's away."

Galina arrives in time to watch the Mazurka. She stops them over the *port de bras*, the tilt of the head, the mazurka step where the front foot has to hit the floor hard and then slide decisively forward. The same problems keep plaguing them: how to differentiate between the mazurka step, a waltz step, and a run, how to get in and out of the wheel, which way to turn. The boys, who are not singled out the way the girls are, become bored and then irritable. Galina ignores them. She is determined every bit of the dance will be done properly and as she taught it. Stubbornly pursuing every movement to correct it, she even demonstrates the figure-eight flourish the girls' hands must make at the end of the dance: "You start the figure eight with the hand going down. You must think about it before. You can't think about it just when you're finishing it."

The Polacca boys don't know when to start moving. Anita tells them calmly, "You will pull it off on the night, but it hasn't really got together yet. It's a very good number if you make something of it." She offers them encouragement, the start of a pep talk, before they all get so tired and bored with repetition that they can't progress at all.

9 November. Three weeks to opening night. The company has gone to Oxford, but no one in the workshops misses them. They need time, not bodies. Reciting like a schoolboy, Edward Percival ticks off the details that together comprise the Czardas dress. Having designed ankle-length skirts, Philip chopped them to calf-length in last week's fittings. Each one has four black net underskirts, and one underskirt has two layers. The hems all hang to the same level, but the three underpetticoats are trimmed with a border of one inch black lace, and the topmost one with three inches of black and gold fringe. "If and when it shows," Edward winks, "it'll be quite nice."

Next he points out ten different braids in Philip's sketch, sixteen rows of braid on each panel of the topskirt, four panels per skirt, six black velvet skirts for two casts of three ladies each. "Janet (Mayo) in the Pattern Room says all this detail is like the cello in the orchestra. You don't actually hear it, but you miss it if it's not there. And she says it's psychologically important for the artist. It's just to give the impression of richness and opulence, all these twiddles and braids. The effect is what you see, not each little detail. You can't see all that from the front."

The dress has no padding on the hips and no basque, and all the skirt goes into

the waist. If you think ballet skirts always fit straight into the waist, look again. Most of them, and *all* tutu skirts, start at the base of a basque, which is the stretch of bodice between the waist and the top of the hip, proportional in length to each dancer's torso. Although this extra length of bodice flatters the dancer's shape and line, it is more functional than decorative. Without it, there would be no place for a man to put his hands while partnering, nowhere they could rest, no way for him to guide and support the woman at her waist. Since there is no partnering in the Czardas, the basque is unnecessary.

Edward pins and talks: "I don't think Joe Public has any idea that people actually *make* the costumes. They just think they appear somehow. And it's always the costumes that get blamed if the dancing's wrong: 'Why didn't you jump higher?' 'Well, my armpit's too tight.' So it's really nice when the artist is pleased with what you've done, and says so. And when the *designer* is pleased and says so . . . that's the supreme accolade. Sometimes you get a certain frock that you feel something for, you put your heart and soul into it. That *Hoffman* one over there is like that, and that was televised. I made a video of it, and when things aren't going so well now, I sometimes just look at the video to remind myself that I *can* do good work.

"The order in which things are done is as important as what is done, and you can't just do the work mechanically. If bones are inserted as soon as a bodice is put together, they must be removed again for the appliqué to be added–not so the braid fits smoother and neater, but because you can't sew through the bones. There's an easy way and a hard way to do things; you find out as you go along. Looking at the sketch, you never know exactly what the problems are going to be.

"I get involved in the costumes. I actually lie awake in bed thinking about how to fit all that sleeve fabric into one tiny armhole. So it's hard to switch from these

79

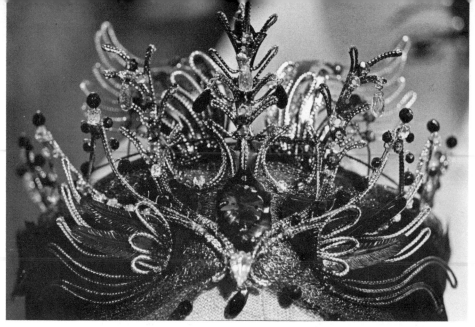

Lac frocks–huge skirts and sleeves, lots of details, curves and twiddles and fringe and lace and intricate appliqué–to doing pleated Greek draperies for *Alceste*. The hands and the machines can do it, but the brain needs adjusting."

Down the hall, Jean Percival is working on Odile. "The one with the black hat on is the baddie," she giggles, "in case you couldn't guess." So far, the headdress includes the basic mesh, frame, millinery wire, tiara, silver wing-shaped twiddles of crin, black feathers, jet beads, jet drops, A/B drops, turquoise faceted sequins, and a few deep turquoise jewels–"Black by itself isn't very interesting, is it?" Also black paint and two-inch decorations of black plastic, shaped like small feathers and lacquered with irridescence. "They don't make those any more, our suppliers tell us. Fortunately I've got a little bag of them put away.

"It's not only the work that takes the time. You've also got to make little drawings of each bit or you'll never be able to reproduce it. Sometimes we have to make them over without an original one for a model."

Jackie is making tiaras for the swans' headdresses, wiring a tiny range of mountain peaks to the frame with fuse wire and stringing individual pearls, or A/B drops, or A/B half-rounds, or faceted rhinestones, onto more fuse wire to attach to the peaks. "Normally you wouldn't do that amount of work on a corps de ballet headdress," Jean admits. "It's hard to say how long a single swan headdress takes to make. With one person working solid eight hours a day, maybe three days. If we don't go to Manchester and something goes wrong, I don't know who they expect to do the work on them. I don't feel confident of them being all right. There's so much on them and they're so difficult to wear. And everyone always blames their headdress. If they fall over on the stage, it's their headdress's fault, so we've got an absolute complex about it. We're just slogging on. If they ever get done I'll be surprised. There are so many processes to go through."

80

Everyone is slogging on. Kim Baker continues to take information in and pass it on as quickly as Philip hands it out. There seems to be no end to it. Kim says, "I've heard that Siegfried is pulled out of the lake at the end. No, it's not a dummy, it's a real person . . . and even if it is a dummy, it has to be dressed." She's also heard that Peter wants to add two couples to the Czardas, but she tells Clare Temple this is impossible. If the first and second cast were all to become the first cast–which is what would happen–every last finished costume would be on stage at once. Lili Sobieralska would have nothing in reserve, no so-called "covers"; in fact, two girls might even be wearing the same dress as the calculations of size and shape have already fitted some of the second cast into costumes made to fit the first cast. From another angle, this means it is simply too late for Peter to have what he wants. Practicality, time and money have taken this particular decision away from him. Time especially is bringing them more and more often to the point where decisions are irrevocable.

Apparently–perhaps intentionally–oblivious of such arbitrary limitations as time and money, Philip visits each of the workrooms to deliver decisions about construction and decoration, braid and lace and trim. Gordon Hutchings asks him about sleeve lining, sashes for Siegfried and the Spanish boys, belts, and braid. Philip sorts all that out, plus topskirts for the Neapolitan girls–maroon, gold tissue and gold fringe–and sequins for the Neapolitan boys' tunics. He draws braid diagrams for Benno and the waltz boys in Act 1, five braids for each, and only selects from what is already in stock. He adds lace to the neckline of Sue

LEFT Act 3 *pas de six* tunic
with some of its braid

BELOW Act 3 *pas de six*
dress in three stages of
completion

Nearly completed
Neapolitan boys' hats

Dempster's "petal" bodices, chooses braid for the loose, swinging panels, and approves the sleeves. Deciding that one red ribbon glares too brightly against the other reds surrounding it, he trims its lower edge with dull gold braid to tone it down. Somewhere in his head, the overall vision is intact; he is now orchestrating the details.

Progress can be seen everywhere. In millinery, the Neapolitan boys' hats now have dyed black feathers, four pheasant and two vulture, and a scarf that is a story in itself. It was meant to be a black lurex with gold through it that Philip chose from a sample, but when they went to order it, they discovered that it isn't made any more. So they got a gold lurex with black through it instead, and are using it on the wrong side. The girls have scattered faceted gold sequins and faceted jet bugle beads all over the lurex, and edged each scarf with flat gold sequins, half an inch wide, 138 of them.

Finished work is piling up at last. "We finished the Czardas and Mazurka boys last week," Jennie Adey boasts. "Mazurka boys have plain flowerpots in black panne with no trim on them at all. Czardas boys get fake Persian lamb with straight vulture feathers in a spray in front, held in place by a gold motif." The way she tosses off the description, you'd almost think the hats had made themselves.

Meanwhile, the company is at the Apollo Theatre in Oxford, dancing *Fille* or *Shrew* by night, rehearsing *Lac* by day. Galina's knee is "not good," and she wears an elastic tube bandage, calf to mid-thigh, for rehearsal. Sherilyn is to replace her in *Fille* so she can rest. Jennie Mills is back in class and says she'll be back on later this week. Peter warns a leaping boy, "Take it easy. Don't do anything to damage yourself even slightly." As opening night draws closer, the slightest injury threatens the production as well as the dancer.

Outside it is crisp and cool, sun shining on the ageless golden stone of ancient colleges. Inside, the theatre is very wide and dark, and decorated with Art Deco railings and jagged slashes of lightning. The dancers do not notice; their vision is reflective, turned onto the stage, the production, themselves. Sue Crow is dancing in lavender sunglasses that match her leotard. Peter has been to Stuttgart to re-set *Giselle* and to Monte Carlo to see about the theatre they will be dancing in at Christmas. He looks calm and rested, but snaps his jacket off and a folding chair open in one impatient gesture, eager to get to work. He turns his attention outward fervently; his mental vision of the ballet is clearer and more tangible after each rehearsal. Desmond sits beside him, then Debbie, Anita, Ron Plaisted and finally Christine Anthony, a guest teacher from the Dutch National Ballet where Peter and Philip did *Sleeping Beauty* together last year. She has just arrived, and will stay through the opening in Manchester.

Act 4. Peter starts talking as soon as the first swan steps from the wings. His comments and Desmond's overlap all afternoon.

Peter: "You're all a bit strutty on the first entrance. You must glide on, gently, feminine." They go back and start again. "Feel the air, feel each other, feel the back arm. You must watch each other all the time, watch your opposite number."

Desmond, picking up the thought: "Look out of the corner of your eye at the next girl–you cannot turn your head to look. And you must get more of a dynamic into the *arabesque*. Push the arm through the air and push the leg up at the same time, and if you do we'll get that lovely feeling of everything rising in the air together and hanging there for just a fraction of a second."

Peter: "Feel it. Make it a bit more physical. Again. Not too wristy."

Desmond: "You must step right on your music, directly on it. You can't drag up onto it. It's so slow and messy if you do. Make sure you step on the beat even if you step softly."

They are stopping now nearly every eight counts, sometimes three or four times over a single step. They stop over doing a *pas de bourrée* in place and not letting any space show between the feet. They stop over the direction of the head on that step–front, Peter decides, rather than angled to the corner. They stop again over being too wristy. They lurch forward bar by bar, faces set. There is, of course, no mirror. They watch their memories, each other, and the eyes of those watching them. "Why do you walk around with that limp arm in front of you and the dangling hand?" Desmond demands. "It looks as if you're carrying your arm on a plate."

Peter has arranged them in a wedge, pointing downstage, and he wants their arms to flow forward, one after the other, in a continuous rolling movement, from the furthest upstage girl to the front. If they each have only one count for the arm movement, it looks too abrupt, too spikey, so he assigns them each two counts. The furthest upstage girl lifts her arm over her head and curves it down at shoulder height in front of her on counts 1 and 2, the next girl in front of her on counts 2 and 3, the next on 3 and 4, ". . . and give a bit of weight in the arm, a bit of fruit, juicy." "Don't be rough on the position, girls," Desmond adds. "Keep the same quality."

The principals wait in the wings, watching, warming up, chatting softly. The entire hour and a half, down on the callsheet for all of Act 4, goes to this one corps dance. Peter says, "Principals, I'm sorry. It has to be right. It has to be right on the night." Galina, Margaret, Sherilyn, David, Alain, Carl, Roland Price as Benno and Grahame Lustig as another Benno and Derek Purnell as another Rothbart or Siegfried, all turn into the shadows without a word and go to lunch. "Use these for thinking rehearsals, please," Peter calls after them.

Does Peter ever eat? He is back on stage before the two couples of the Neapolitan dance appear to work with him. They run through it, at breakneck speed as always, and Peter takes some steps out and puts some others in. You can see the outlines of all the earlier versions in the impulses they must now throttle. Nick Ringham tries to jump much too high in much too little time; where the jump once was, Peter has inserted a small beat, which he wants done very fast and close to the ground. After an hour, he claps his hands and nods once: "That, let's hope, is the last change I'm going to make. Until you've got the costumes on."

The principals gather slowly for Act 1, which Peter plans to run for their benefit with the corps dancers present but not actually dancing. As they begin, he says, "I know, I wanted to do motivations." He has not mentioned the word before, but having now said it, he also brings his full attention to it. For over an hour, he gives detailed, specific acting notes while they dance:

"Benno, you've got to come on all excited. You're the one who's organizing the whole thing. Come on and be bold, earthy, into the ground." Returning the character of Benno to the ballet is another of Peter's decisions about the drama and logic of the story, and Roland's evident talent made him a logical choice for the first cast. " And, Prince, come on thinking, and then stop and look around at all this.

"You must all resist the temptation to do *port de bras* and wave your arms about. Simpler is always best. One gesture is stronger than all that waving.

"David, when you take the crossbow it's just polite. You're not the slightest bit interested.

"When the Queen is announced . . . well, she's the cause of all your problems. Benno's got to play 'Oh Christ, here she comes' and then I want you two to show that you're very good friends, that the Prince has confided in Benno.

"Queen, you must be very sad, very sad. You're in deepest mourning. And you know Siegfried's sad too. And you're very worried about him—you know what a rough time lies ahead of him." He stages the greeting between them so it is very tender, all drooping lines, grief and affection from both of them.

Sami Saidi, the second cast Queen Mother, is moving upstage of Anita through the whole act. Madeleine Sheehan is here as well, trying to appear casual as she waits eagerly for Act 1 to be over. On the original cast list, she is the

Act 1: "She's the cau[se]
of all your problems[."]
David Ashmole and
Anita Landa

"Show that you're
very good friends."
(left to right) Roland
Price and David
Ashmole

last, the tenth, listed to learn and cover Odette, but Marion, Petal Miller, Jennie Mills and Siobhan Stanley, all of whom precede her, are all off. Petal is the latest to fall; she has food poisoning and never got to Oxford at all.

They move on to Act 2. Galina hangs back, guarding her knee and her nerves. Margaret is in front with Alain. Desmond cautions her, "Be very careful to mime only with one arm. Leave the other one by your tutu. If both of them are moving, the audience doesn't know where to look." He wants her solo "smooth as whipped cream." She goes straight on to Act 3; now Peter wants her to think of each *renversé* in Odile's solo as a breath rather than a balance in order to keep from going static. And "What is the accent on the *fouettés*, down or up? It should be down." Time does not pass. The stage remains bright, the dancers continue to dance. "You've got five minutes," Peter announces suddenly. "You can just do the last act *pas de deux* and then you'll have done it all." David Ashmole lets his knees buckle and collapses in a mock swoon at the thought of more, yet another *pas de deux*. "I said I'd make it up to you," laughs Peter, referring to their patience that morning. And they go ahead, since they have the five minutes, and dance the final *pas de deux* too.

16 November. Two weeks to opening night. Monday morning in the London Opera Centre. "Only four and a half days to go," says Robin. "The truck comes Friday." *Swan Lake* will travel, both to Manchester and on tour, in four "wagons," forty foot lorries owned and driven by Radcliffe Transport. One will carry only electrics: 150 lamps, a lighting board, cables, coloured gel, all boxed and barrelled. The other three will take the entire set, drops, flats and columns–broken down, naturally–and the wicker skips of costumes and shoes.

But there's plenty of work to do before the lorries arrive. The backcloth for Acts 2 and 4 is hanging on stage where the cinema screen once hung. What started as a huge blank canvas has now had chunks of its solidity replaced with sharkstooth gauze so that Siegfried and Odette, reunited in death, can be seen through it at the end of Act 4. The remaining canvas has been sprayed with water to tauten it, and then given two coats of dense black paint by hand and a layer of silver texture by roller. "This silver will shine up like a pussycat's fur in the moonlight," says Mike, admiring it.

Toward the bottom of the cloth gleam the watery shapes of a lake. After Mike drew them on the white canvas in charcoal, Robin painted them with Decadex, a fire-resistant agent that smooths the cloth beneath it and lends a shiny surface to ordinary paint applied on top of it. Robin has varnished that surface for an even higher gloss. "Philip may even have to add glitter to the lake shapes–otherwise they may not read as shiny," Mike explains. "You only get that shine if the light hits them at an angle."

The columns loom, assembled to various heights, from every corner of the workroom. When they first arrived from the Old Vic Annexe, paper rope had to be added as extra moulding. Then they were "gunged up" by hand. The "gunge or glop–that's what I call it," says Dave, "is a thick paste of plaster powder,

Texturing on colum▌

water and black dye. Once you've slapped that down everywhere, you've got texture for design purposes, and you've lost all your rough edges–everything has a uniform surface." Black paint covers the gunge, and silver paint is dragged over the black so the peaks of the texturing catch the silver but the valleys don't. Mike points out that the downstage columns look blacker and the upstage ones more silvery. "The columns might look beautiful or they might look like a graveyard. You can't really know until you light them. A little silver onstage can go a long way–it can come up like a lot of little mirrors."

Tuesday. While work may be winding down on *Lac* in the paint shop, it's just beginning at the prop shop in Killick Street where two carpenters, one labourer and nine propmakers are employed full time by the Opera House. "And I double sometimes as Head of Department," says Michael Whiteley, shaking my hand. He is slim, fair and wiry, and comes from a circus family. "We hadn't started on *Lac* until today because we didn't have the room. By the time we got the show from Philip, we were well into *Alceste* and there was no way anyone could stop. This is the first week anyone could work on it.

"*Swan Lake* is very unreal and fantastic, fairy time, lots of silver glitter. *Alceste* is very real, very true to life, and if a detail is wrong, the designer will say so. It's hard to know if it's better to have a designer hanging around your neck or not–it depends very much if you've worked for him before. With *Alceste*, it *has* been good, because it's a designer we haven't worked with before and he wanted things very precise. We're doing *Swan Lake* on the cuff and we've only got five

88

days to do it, but I've worked with Philip and I know what he wants. All ballets end up with glitter on them anyway."

He shows me hexagonal lanterns made of half inch plywood and hardboard filigree, and they are complete. All the sides are there, nothing is faked or missing. "We don't know how our things are going to be used, so we must build them all, go the whole hog. Lucky we haven't got a lot of hand props or they'd never get built. And the table he wanted would have been two weeks worth of carpentry and another two weeks of prop work. That's out of the question. So, OK, if we can't do the table, what shall we do? Well, let's make a simple table and put a tablecloth on it. That's only about three days carpentry work.

"For the tablecloth, Philip brought in a picture of a figured carpet which has to be reproduced at the scale of one inch to one foot. He said, 'Make it black, grey and silver.'" So they bought a figured cotton fabric with a beige and black basketweave pattern, and decorated it with grey satin and two silver braids. The curlicues of the pattern went on in "p.v.a.", polyvinyl coating which was mixed with silver powder and squirted through a syringe like icing on a cake.

Philip has also asked for a silver centrepiece, several tiers high, for the party in Act 1. To set them on the right track, he gave them a photograph of an ornate Victorian cakestand, thick with vines and cherubs and bunches of silver grapes, from the Crystal Palace Exhibition of 1890. Working from that and a sketch

Decorating the Act 1 tablecloth

89

Underlying
construction of Act 1
centrepiece

drawn to the scale of one inch to six inches, one of the propmakers is busily encrusting a plastic cakestand with three-inch plastic dolls, modelling clay, and drips and blobs from a glue gun. "You shop for stuff depending on whether it's cheaper to buy it or make it," says Mike. "Because this has to be so quick, it's cheaper to buy little plastic men for this–they're all out of *Star Wars*–and muck 'em about a bit."

Or you use what you've already got around. "We had a mould already made for the *Alceste* torches. So we ran off a few extra, stuck them together, painted them up a bit, and they became lances for *Swan Lake*." Or, if need be, you adapt the designs. "If we have the time and the money, I'll make anything they ask for. It doesn't matter to me. Philip wants eight chairs for the ballroom–we pad them with foam rubber on the seat and the back, just for the sake of the dancers who sit on them. From the drawing I've got, they're supposed to have fringe from the seat to the floor, but it's too costly." So he's cut a big diamond canvas throw which has gone to the paint frame at the Opera House. They'll cut seven more like it, paint them all the same colour as the Act 3 set, and send them back here to be tacked onto the chairs like loose covers. "You won't see much more of the chair than its general shape."

"It is rather unusual to make a show in a week, especially a new show," one of the girls comments. But the unusual is commonplace in this business. As Mike says, "If you're really professional about it, you just get on with making it."

Wednesday. In the Pattern Room, Louise is getting on with it. "The trouble with tights is that there are so many of them and each boy's got two pair for every role he does. Because everyone's doing so much, switching and replacing, I've automatically bought two pair of black for each boy in the company. I've also got two pair dyed for each boy that is down to dance each role, no matter what cast he is. It means we won't run out for years, and if the same boy dances matinée and evening, running wardrobe doesn't have to wash and dry tights between performances, so it's very good for maintenance too."

Black suede gauntlets are expected at any moment from Devon–that is, Louise *hopes* they'll arrive at any moment: "We haven't used this company before, but I couldn't trace the company we always did use. Philip decided on the shape, and we have to decorate them. They're made in average sizes for one full cast and one spare." Her list includes Rothbart, Queen, court ladies, court gents, court officials, nuns, pages, guards . . . a total of forty pairs.

She gladly leaves the lists on her desk to accompany Philip into Betterton Street where Colin McKenzie and Carl Bonn have been making Rothbart's two costumes in their own workroom. They parade the Act 3 cloak first; it's like a stained glass window of deep reds and golds and swirly patterns of braid that they have laid out, as Carl says, "so you get that lovely art nouveau feeling." Since Rothbart must shed this cloak in seconds to reveal his true, evil identity, it must be closed around him with something that will fly open quickly and easily– buttons, for example, would be useless. The logical choice would be Velcro, which rips open with a mere tug, but instead, to avoid the noise tearing Velcro makes, Colin and Carl have closed the front of the cloak with a string of snap fasteners. "They sound very loud when demonstrated," they admit, "but much quieter than we all know the Velcro would be."

The costume for Act 2 and 4 is dense with black leaves that twine over a body stocking and trail off it in eerie silken tatters. "Every single leaf has been lined," Philip notes with appreciation. "Otherwise they'd look like death in three weeks," Carl murmurs modestly, obviously pleased that Philip is so pleased.

Out on the pavement again, Philip remarks, "You give them the designs, the fabric and the braid, and they'll just work it out. They're so good that they're almost insulted if you give them diagrams. And they'll also come to the first fitting with everything nearly made and the braid pinned all over it, but with plenty of room to manoeuvre. The dancers will look at it and say, 'Oh, it's going to be gorgeous,' and then you won't get another peep out of them and you can go ahead and do precisely as you like. They're the best in Europe, probably in the world."

Thursday. The gold fringe for the maroon Neapolitan topskirts arrived yesterday. The suede gauntlets have arrived too, and Louise is gluing labels that say only *Lac* and an act number into all the cuffs. That's the only distinction they need since they're identical otherwise, size small for the girls and pages and size medium for all the boys.

Jean Percival reports, "I've got three Odettes finished now and two Odiles, and there are two swans completely finished. All the mesh is on the frames, so we know there's just enough to go around."

Jennie Adey reports, 'We'll finish it right enough, but we'll have to take it up to Manchester with us Tuesday or Wednesday. There's no way we can have this done in time to pack on Saturday. All the basic bits are here. It's only a question of assembling them. We'd be finished now if we hadn't had all the *Alceste*."

Edward Percival uses the identical words: "It's just a question of assembling everything. And of course I've run out of braid again, so I'll have no two skirts the same. This one skirt panel and four pairs of sleeves and all the bits that go along the bottom will have to be different. But it's not their fault; I blame it all on the Church of England. Well, it's ecclesiastical braid, after all. It's all gone on the Archbishop of Canterbury. We'll have to go 'round and unpick his." The girls don't laugh; they may not even hear him. They're too busy to listen. There are tickets lying under the gold lamé, and in Gordon's workroom, the Pattern Room, millinery, everywhere, for Tuesday morning's dress rehearsal of *Alceste*. Everyone's dying to go, if they're not in Manchester by then, but they don't know if they'll have the time.

November 23. Five days to opening night. Manchester. The Palace Theatre is enormous; two huge balconies and a total of 1,937 seats, an opera house in the old, grand style. Designed by Robert Matcham and opened in 1891 with a ballet called *Cleopatra*, its original opulence has recently been restored with red velvet,

Czardas dress

dull gold paint, and globes like the flames of torches in the sconces. Back of house is new as well, and slick with white paint. There is one lift, boxed by a rectangular staircase, connecting six floors of dressing rooms, each floor with its number hugely painted opposite the lift door. It is a bright, clean, wholly impersonal facility that could be an airport or an office block, except for the long counters of dressing tables and steel-edged make-up mirrors framed in lights. Upper-floor dressing rooms have been assigned to staff and extras; wardrobe and management have their own rooms slightly closer to the stage level, and there is a canteen with a Roadrunner video game that plays day and night. You can smell chips frying as you climb the stairs.

The company has already moved in. It doesn't take them long to spread out their shoes and make-up, and wedge photos and cartoons around the mirrors. In the course of a single cup of tea in the canteen, before the afternoon's rehearsals start, you can easily pick up the latest company news. Carl has the all-time winning score on the Roadrunner game. Russell Maliphant has been given a contract with the company, effective last Friday. Which was also the first orchestra rehearsal for *Swan Lake*. Stephen Wicks has food poisoning and is off tonight. Jennie Mills and Petal Miller both returned to work in Newcastle last week. "I'm dreaming about *Swan Lake*," Jennie admits. "I'm not doing Big Swans any more, but I'm doing Jane Billson's place in the corps—she's now a lady-in-waiting. I was put in last week, for the first time since Plymouth, and I did all four acts. I'm shocked at the number of mistakes I made, and still worried about the number I'm going to make."

They're all a bit worried. Nikki Katrak's nerves make her chatter: "We're not used to rehearsing things so much, so all these rehearsals will be like doing six shows in three days. It's quite shattering, especially if you're not used to doing a lot of pointework. All the swans' dancing is on pointe and we were wearing hard shoes to take the strain off it, but Anita said we couldn't wear stiff shoes because we couldn't all be clattering about. We said, 'We can't wear soft shoes to rehearse in. All that pointe work hurts so much.' And the other thing was that in rehearsal last week, I fell and Mandy-Jayne fell because we were both wearing new shoes. And after the two of us went, Peter said we had to forget about new shoes because we couldn't risk having anyone go off. So the joke was, you had to do *échappés* in the aisle of the train to break your shoes in between cities." Her eyes shine; she's excited too.

Sandra Madgwick, a cygnet and a Neapolitan girl and less than a year out of the School, says as much: "The tour is exciting for me because it's my first one. I haven't got bored with it or depressed yet. And *Swan Lake* is very exciting because I haven't been in the long classical things before, and I've got good things to dance."

The extras, three women and twelve men, are even more thrilled. Privileged members, however briefly, of a select society, they are escorted through the one door that leads to the stage and down the iron stairs to join the rehearsal. Too shy to take a step without Peter's direction, they cluster nervously together. He is carefully polite to them at first, and then treats them casually, exactly as he treats his dancers, which flatters them into exactly the professional behaviour he needs from them. Perhaps he does it intentionally; more likely it is simply another aspect of his gift for fusing bodies and movement.

Before they begin on Act 3, Brian Ferguson, head of men's wardrobe, drapes Ron Plaisted in his sumptuous Master of Ceremonies robe. The dancers gasp, and sidle up to him one by one all afternoon to stroke and admire it, like a succession of Giselles. Waiting for instructions on the cold draughty stage, sometimes four, sometimes five of them huddle under its train. Ron isn't even aware of it, they sit so still.

Although no one else but Anita Landa is yet in costume, the production already fills corners of the stage that have always been empty. There are banners to herald the Queen Mother's entrance, two nuns and two monks attending her, and torches-jammed-together as lances in the hands of nervous extras. Peter's voice stirs up the mêlée, coaxing and prodding at it to unify its still disparate elements. The more his vision materializes, the more eagerly he pushes it toward completion.

"Everyone standing around, when the Prince comes on you must all talk, react. You know, he's late to the party, there's a bit of trouble. And the Queen must greet him like 'At last you're here. Go and take your proper place.'" He cannot sit back and watch; in another moment, he's on his feet again, pointing, gesturing, his face alight. "Everyone, as the Hungarian Princess passes . . . well, she *is* a princess so you must do . . . well, don't do a full ballet bow, but you must bow. And when the Polish Princess comes on, I want you all to bow at the same time, and the time will be when she gives her hand to her ambassador." Everyone walks; no one dances. It looks a total muddle, like a crowd scene in a school play. Peter is undaunted: "After the Princesses dance, you must all start to move in because you want to know who's going to be chosen." They move, but only mechanically, too distracted by the cold, the costumes and the massive set–"It looks just like Gormanghast"–to become involved.

Desmond is waiting upstage to make his first Rothbart entrance in the glittering cloak Colin and Carl have made him. He can foresee the impact it will have; there is a sly, delighted half-grin on his face, which could just as well be Rothbart's grin, and he is chewing gum.

"'*Who* is *this*?' That's your reaction to Rothbart and Odile . . . I've got another fifteen minutes? And I should have done Act 1, shouldn't I? Well, I can't." Peter goes straight on to stage the revelation of Rothbart, instructing the Spanish entourage to remove his cloak while hiding his body upstage of them, "and we don't want to see it happen. It must be magic." That's the last point he gets to make; he had called Act 3 at 4:00, Act 1 at 5:00, and the time is gone. At 5:30 the crew takes over on stage to strike the *Lac* columns and set up for the 7:30 performance of *Shrew*.

The dancers scatter—to nap, eat, shower, clean their pointe shoes. With a little time to spare, conductor Barry Wordsworth talks about *Lac* over his canteen dinner: "It's up to me to show Peter what all the options are. I tell him what I think musically and he tells me if it fits in with what he wants to do. His contact, as mine, was 'Let's get back to what Tchaikovsky intended originally,' which sounds very noble in these days of echt-research and authenticity. Then you find out it was a flop, and when it was revived twenty years later the music was re-composed and the order changed. There are whole chunks you can cut out—there's a good four hours of music there if you play cover to cover without intervals—but if you take eight bars out, you've got to take the eight-bar repeat out as well. It's like the classical façade of a building: if you take a column off this side, you've got to lop it off the other side too.

"We looked at the possibility of going back to the original original, which puts the Act 2 *pas de deux*, the cygnets and the waltzes in a different order. What we all know and love is not the original version at all, but it does make sense musically and that's how it's been got to. The Black and White Swan *pas de deux* are part of our heritage. You certainly don't tamper with those simply for the sake of a new production.

"Peter's point was to make the story as clear as possible. How many productions start off with a cortège? This one does. It hasn't been staged yet, but it will be, with music from the end of the overture. We didn't even have to change the music. A great tragedy has descended on them all. In other productions, it usually happens before the curtain goes up.

"Every note of our production, even with our alterations, has been *Swan Lake* music. The previous Act 4, at the Garden, had Drigo's orchestration of the *Valse*

Black Swan *pas de deux*. Margaret Barbieri and Desmond Kelly

Bluette in it—a happy, jolly number, so wrong for *Swan Lake*—and a piano piece called *Un Poco di Chopin* by Tchaikovsky. Peter swung over to the original Act 4, with heavy cuts, minus *Valse Bluette* and *Un Poco di Chopin*, and with the addition for the *pas de deux* of one of the diverts from Act 3, which had to be transposed to fit. We do all the apotheosis music, uncut, and other little bits I'm very glad to have in, which we *have* because Galina remembered what she'd danced to them.

"Then there was the question of the boy's solo at the end of Act 1, where Covent Garden still does Nureyev's. The music is from the divert in Act 1, what Covent Garden calls the *pas de trois* but should really be a *pas de quatre* with the Prince as part of it. Tchaikovsky wrote that sad music as the second of the four variations, so the Prince *must* have been in it.

"This is our largest touring orchestra so far. Basic touring size is forty-six, *Lac*

Siegfried's solo in the *pas de quatre*: Carl Myers

orchestra is fifty-six—six extra strings, two trumpets, one flute, one percussion. It's still not quite big enough, but one hopes it still sounds like Tchaikovsky. Ideally one would like more strings. If you heard it in the concert hall you'd have sixteen first violins, so I tell ours everyone has to play for two."

At the next table, one of the girls is wide-eyed and breathless: "Have you seen the costumes down in the scene dock? It's like Aladdin's cave."

24 November. Tuesday. 9:00 a.m. Now that the set is built, painted, and assembled in one place, it must be lit. As a result, immediately after last night's performance, the stage crew struck *Shrew*, erected *Lac*, and began—as their callsheet put it—to "Set, Focus and Light A. 1 *Lac*, then Set and Focus A. 2." They worked from half-hour for *Shrew*, 7:00 p.m., until 5:00 this morning, and are walking back in right now to light Act 2. They have the stage to themselves until 11:30. John B. Read sits in the middle of the darkened theatre with his lighting plot of the lamps' positions spread on a makeshift desk laid over the backs of the seats. He holds the colours he's assigned to each lamp in his head, and calls for the mix he wants on each cue without referring to any list except the one in his memory. Having previously watched rehearsals at the Wells and during the tour, he now has roughly four days to determine where the light from more than sixty lamps will fall—and when and what colour and for how long—at every moment of the ballet.

Robin Snow stayed in the theatre until three in the morning, finishing little bits of painting, blacking the braces on the leaf flats, darkening the chair covers for Act 3 which came out a different shade of red from the set and the backcloth.

Sherilyn Kennedy as the
Hungarian Princess

He is carrying a small plastic bag of black sequins that Kim brought him "in case
I couldn't get any glitter for the lake. But I managed to find some, so now I've
got both."

In production wardrobe on the fourth floor, Louise is scissoring the hem of
the Polish Princess's black and gold topskirt into points. Kim has gone to Red
Star to collect mourning cloaks and jet necklaces. They were both here until
3:00 a.m. beading the swans' topskirts; Philip stayed at it until 5:00. Jane
Cowood is knotting elasticized gold cord into macramé lace for the neck and
sleeves of the Princesses' tutus, and each knot will have a bronze sequin stitched
to it. Jean Percival and Alison arrived at 10:30 last night: "We finished them all
but we've both got streaming colds. Just keep your fingers crossed." The gloves
are here too, all trimmed with gold motifs and silver braid.

10:20 a.m. The corridors fill with girls on their way to barre in everyday
leotards of all colours and swan headdresses. "No one told us to come to class in
make-up and headdress, but we've only got a quarter of an hour between," says
Janis Parsons. As the rehearsal calls for sets, lights, props and costumes, the girls
will have to put their tutus on for the first time in those fifteen minutes. Whatever they can do to save themselves time after class, they have already done.

11:30 a.m. After wearing the headdresses for an hour, the girls complain that
they have all been made too small, without taking account of their coiled-up
hair. They're wearing them at every conceivable angle, from high on the hair to
low across the forehead. As they waddle down the narrow iron stairs to the
stage, frowning, tugging at the elastic shoulderstraps on their swan tutus,

99

Michael Soffe switches on the loudspeaker to say, "Ladies of the corps, the top layer of your tutus is very fragile. Please be careful not to catch them or brush against lights, pillars or scenery." The girls' faces sour further.

All of Act 2 is dressed, including the Act 1 waltz boys who are hunting with Siegfried and Benno at the top of the act. Stephen Wicks: "It's gorgeous. I love it all." Mark Welford: "Feel the belt. It weighs a ton." Reactions all week will split between the objective and purely practical–Can I dance in this? Is it secure? Can it hurt me or anyone else?–and the spontaneously enthusiastic.

They begin Act 2, Galina and David with Desmond as Rothbart, the opening night cast. "Desmond, don't lie down each time. Just lean against the pillar," calls Peter from out front. Now that he can see the costume of leaves and the pillar and the leaf carpet covering the stairs and the light, he can also see the gaps between his ideas and the physical form they've taken in rehearsal. Some movements will simply look wrong, others unnecessary, and a few will be invisible. He will make changes that he could not possibly anticipate until all the elements came together. Some of the notes he'd give anyway: "All eyes must be down," during the *pas de deux*, or "You've got to move your arms sharp on the three plonks before your waltz, girls. Your arms are waving all over." But, "Cygnets, the *pas de chat* are not showing up at all" could mean that they're simply not jumping enough or that in the tutus they'll have to jump even higher, clearer, than he would ordinarily demand or the step will be lost in the skirt.

The swans break ranks, stand flat on their feet, and talk about spacing their lines while the two Big Swans dance centrestage. In her Odette headdress and grey running suit, handbag over arm, Galina shows them yet again how to flap their wings. The last exit of swans backs up onstage like an impatient bus queue. There's very little room to get off in the upstage wing, and they can't see where

Repairing the beadwork on a swan bodice

they're going once they squeeze through it. John Read promises a lamp will be rigged.

Although you can't hear them fall because of the music, pearls are dropping off the bodices and topskirts like rain. They are even more dangerous than most litter on stage because they are so hard to see. All afternoon, the girls in Act 1 will pick them up whenever they stop dancing.

"And I've got a dent in my head from that headdress, and such a headache," one swan moans at lunch. "You're supposed to wear them right down on your hairline–doesn't matter what it feels like, you must wear them there. Even if you die! The pain! the suffering!" She jokes to keep her spirits up, to laugh her headache away, since she has no choice but to do exactly as she is told.

2:30 p.m. Act 1 is in costume for the first time, and now the boys are swept into the panoply. The waltz boys are slim and elegant in grey-green-blue velvet tunics, the Polacca boys solemn and mysterious in stiff, brocaded capes like coats. Iain Webb breathes, "Aren't these wonderful? Have you ever seen anything like them?" Grahame Lustig responds, "Boring costumes, aren't they? Ordinary. Basic Gothic court made to measure." They are so unaccustomed to looking glamourous that they can hardly express their delight.

But one boy complains that the gauntlets are too big: "There *are* things called fittings and tape measures." Louise just laughs at his serious expression: "Hard enough to get hold of you for costume fittings without worrying about glove fittings." And Madeleine Sheehan mutters, "The court ladies' shoes are a bit

Act 1: the Polacca

small, but that's nothing to the weight of the dress." Like the Queen, she wears a huge dress and train over a hoop, trailing velvet sleeves, and two long black veils. It will be impossible *not* to notice that the court is in deepest mourning.

Now that he has extras, Peter can stage the cortège. He creates the procession in mere minutes: the dead king's coffin and crown followed by Siegfried, his weeping mother, nuns, priests, courtiers, all of them shrouded in black. Months later, when he has time to talk, Peter will say, "I knew we must start with a funeral procession to establish the whole thing. Nobody I talked to about it thought it would work. They were all dead against it, everyone. But it was easy to try—it only took ten minutes to stage—and if it hadn't worked, you'd just cut it out." Now all he says is ". . . and move to your places, very smoothly and quietly. You just vanish."

The waltz starts. "Will you take those roses out of the way?" he calls politely from the darkness. His tone says "There's a good idea that has to go." They can't shower the Prince with rose petals when he comes on if they then have to dance on them. Peter asks David to repeat his entrance, and tells the girls to curtsey to him when he comes on. Throughout these staging rehearsals, the principals will work like film actors, turning emotion and character on and off as if both ran from taps.

The waltz starts again, boldly, and then deteriorates in a stream of errors. None of the boys can pirouette properly, and the skirts keep catching on the decorative buckles on their belts. Chenca's headdress almost puts Mark Welford's eye out. No one marks a step, but all the girls are gasping for breath. Are the dresses too tight? Is the dance too fast? Are they beginning to panic? It's just as bad the second time they do it. Peter doesn't waste time giving notes; why bother to tell them what they already know?

He also doesn't panic. He has too much to do, and not a moment to spare. "Can we get more people downstage to mask the table before the Queen comes on?" One of the boys answers, "It's a bit difficult with the dresses." There are court ladies in the corner already, in front of the table, but only a few since each stands at the centre of the wide circumference of her skirt. One of them steps backward on her train, and sits down hard.

Peter restages the entrance of the Queen Mother, attendant nuns and court officials. Although he still wants everyone to move as quickly as in rehearsal clothes, he must make allowance for the length and weight of their trailing costumes. For the first time, the court officials are carrying books with painted pictures of the Princesses in them to show the Prince. Like a magician, Peter conjures up moves for the Prince, for the officials, for the trains of their robes—nicknamed at once "the walking duvets"—and for the books too since he wants the pictures clearly seen by the audience.

The Polacca boys dance smoothly and look amazingly grand considering they've been wearing their heavy capes for two and a half hours while waiting to dance in them. When they break at nearly 5:00, the second cast called for the

afternoon has not put a foot on stage. "Never mind," says Lili Griffiths, fluffing the wide skirt of her *pas de quatre* tutu, "it means we'll get a proper call another day."

Henry Menary, who is the wigs department on tour all by himself, is combing, clipping and shaping while everyone else is eating. He will leave the company for a new job in South Africa shortly after *Lac* opens. "I wasn't going to come on this tour, but Clare Temple convinced me I should because the company needed someone they knew to help get *Swan Lake* on." His little room is warmed by the hotbox and glaring with fluorescent light for his fine work, and he has a calm answer for everything. Why was Denis Bonner alone wearing a dark wig and beard in the Polacca? "The decision was only made two or three weeks ago that they *would* have wigs, so they had to be taken out of stock and fitted. The Act 1 wigs that I got from stock—and they usually come from a dead opera—looked like this one: long, loose waves. It's really rather feminine, so I got permission from Philip to cut and style it to suit our quite masculine boys. The one Denis was wearing this afternoon was the prototype and it got approved, so now I can make the other five." He says there are also beards and moustaches for the Polacca courtiers and for the court officials, Czardas boys, Mazurka boys, Neapolitan boys and Ron Plaisted as Master of Ceremonies. The Neapolitan girls will have wigs too. The steadiness in his voice lulls you into thinking that urgency hasn't yet been invented.

Downstairs in production wardrobe, an alarm clock is ringing in a carrier bag: "It's Susanna's. She set it for 6:00 to wake herself up." Gordon's assistant Fay only acknowledges the time by saying, "We've got a lot of work to do before tomorrow. We'll work late tonight," which may be the understatement of the week.

Jean and Alison have been making headdress repairs based on complaints, but they are now concocting a tiny white swan headdress as a gift for Philip. They will stay to see Black Swan on stage tomorrow afternoon, and then leave.

During *Shrew*, Ann Carol falls coming down the iron stairs into the wings. As Kate, Chenca throws such a realistic tantrum during the first wedding that her necklace flies off into the wings. One of Petruchio's bizarre servants misses an entrance, and Grahame Lustig somehow manages to play two servants at once. Karen Donovan has terribly swollen glands, but the doctor says she's all right. Clare French says she feels sick all the time, "but it may just be excitement." Anita says, "It's been a very fraught day. They're all getting a bit weepy." Maybe *that's* the understatement of the week.

25 November. Wednesday. 9:00 a.m. John B. Read goes back to lighting Act 4. He and the crew set, focussed and lit Act 3 after *Shrew* last night, and set and focussed Act 4, leaving only the cues to be done this morning. They only worked until about 4:00 a.m., which they consider a great improvement over the night before.

Jennie Adey drove up last night—"I couldn't have come on the train with the amount of stuff I had"—and arrived just after the show. She has brought four Spanish girls' hats, two of them still unfinished, a cardinal's hat, a box of beards, one Czardas dress and a bag of braid for Gordon. "And a partridge in a pear tree," sings Edward, who has just arrived this morning, having come on the train with one girl and three frocks. He says he finished in plenty of time, at 6:00 yesterday evening, and had a good night's sleep. Jean and Alison are also sitting in production wardrobe, but they have not put on the white coveralls they wear for work clothes. They have finished their work; they are waiting to see Odile.

Kim cheers them all with the story of the court officials' capes. The "walking duvets" are truly magnificent, black and gold brocade splashed with gold and brown, blue and black, lined with dark blue watered silk and caught up at odd angles so they envelop the boys who wear them—Derek, Russell and Douglas Vardon. It seems that after the cloaks first went on stage yesterday, Philip suggested to Kim that they be cut from the show. He thought them too big and too sumptuous against the Queen Mother's sombre black; he called it "a design mistake." Knowing all the time and work and money that had gone into them, Kim thought fast and said, "Why don't we turn them inside out?" "Brilliant," exclaimed Philip, and on they went. He then asked Galina, "What do you think of the court officials?" and she answered, "Darling, I didn't notice them. But their hats are too big." Everyone roars. It is the perfect wardrobe story: although the "duvets" each contain more than twenty-five square yards of the richest fabrics, they are, to a dancer, all but invisible.

Louise hardly smiles. She has her own problems. The company was originally told they could have "costumes as available" for the Friday morning dress rehearsal. "But that rehearsal is now down on the callsheet as a photocall," which means everyone must be fully costumed. "But they'll be in the costumes for two complete runthroughs on Thursday, so Friday will be the only time we can get them ready for the opening. We'll have quite a lot of pressing and steaming to do too. I don't know when we're going to do it."

Warm-up barre today, like yesterday, is in the foyer at the circle level, which is thickly carpeted and hung with heavy drapes. There is no piano, no mirror, no heat. But the crew is lighting Act 4 on stage until the rehearsal, and there is nowhere else for Christine Anthony to give a barre. The dancers continue arriving for ten minutes after she has begun. They are breathless and embarrassed at their tardiness, but they only know their way around the *back* of the theatre. The front is a maze to them, and no one has provided a map.

11:20 a.m. Ten more minutes to yank off their wet leotards and, slightly more cautiously, yank on their tutus. Franziska Merky calls out, "Has anyone said anything about our tights?" They all think the pink of their tights clashes with the creamy ivory of their tutus. Since everyone wears different brands, according to her own preference, the pinks even differ from one swan to the next. Franziska wriggles into a very pink pair on purpose: "Well, you've got to make them notice," and someone else suggests wearing "a blue-y pink pair" for the contrast. They don't want to be issued white ones; they just want to be required to wear the same thing.

At every rehearsal now, the critical eyes observe the action from a distance. Peter sits near the glow of the lamp on John Read's temporary desk in the centre of the stalls. Since yesterday's Act 2 runthrough, he has had a microphone in his hand, which amplifies his thoughts and his control as well as his voice. It allows him to work like the director of a silent film; he speaks right through the music and the action, changing both as they occur and then modifying the changes as he sees them take shape. Whatever he doesn't say aloud to the dancers, he murmurs to Alison, his assistant, who takes notes. Philip and/or Kim and/or Louise sit nearby, also whispering constantly and taking notes.

John Read speaks into his headset; his comments, like Peter's, produce immediate results: "Follow spot, get on the legs for a minute . . . no, the dancers' legs." The hanging velours that divide the wings are also called legs. "And while we're talking about that great rugby scrum involving the Prince, Rothbart and her Ladyship in Act 4, I want to contrive to keep Rothbart lit as much as the Prince. In a funny way, he's just as important there. It's really a three-lamp situation, but we haven't got them so we'll have to do what we can." His job is not simply a matter of electricity, but of understanding Peter's intention and enhancing it.

11:30 a.m. Act 4 now opens with dry ice, although, John Read mutters, "Where the dry ice is going to come from in Act *3*, we have yet to find out." Sandra snags her tutu in the upstage foliage as she turns a tight corner. Galina's bodice sprays jewels in all directions, and when she tries to escape Rothbart, her hand smacks the wings on his helmet. Fleeing up the centre steps to leap to her death, she pauses dramatically before she jumps, peers offstage, and sees

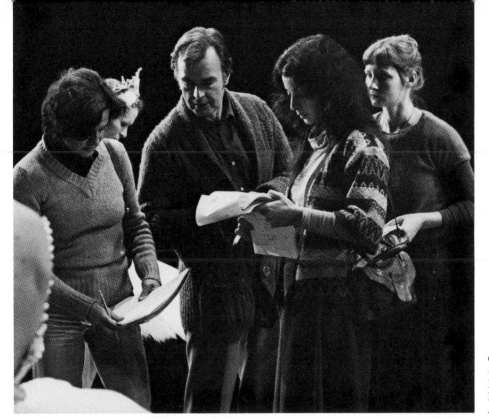

Giving notes onstage:
(left to right) Anita
Landa, Peter Wright,
Deborah Chapman,
Alison Palmer

Act 4. Galina Samsov
and Desmond Kelly

106

nothing but blackness and empty space. Now, Odette may be willing to die, but Galina most definitely is not. So she lets herself down by hand, squatting on the platform gingerly and then sliding off into the darkness, feet first. Seeing her difficulty and sensing her unspoken distress, Peter presses Derek Purnell and Nick Millington into service—henceforth, every Odette will be assigned two "catchers."

In the Siegfried–Rothbart fight, David collides with a flock of flapping swans who are just doing as they've been told. Extricating himself at last, he runs, jumps, dies. The body Benno pulls from the lake, and carries toward the foot-lights as the apotheosis music swells and the vision of the lovers appears, is Michael O'Hare's, clothed in a Siegfried Act 3 tunic that is too large for him. Michael will also play the dead Siegfried when Desmond is the live one, and Russell will stand in as the corpse for Alain or Carl.

Before the second runthrough of the act, this time with Sherilyn and Carl, Peter revises and rehearses the spacing for the storm. He then asks John Read, "When we get the storm, with the lightning going and all, could we have a little more change of light? Because suddenly the wind is blowing up." Within a single sentence, they refer both to the instruments of illusion, the means, and the illusion itself, the ends. As long as you know the context, it makes perfect sense;

Act 4: the apotheosis

Act 4. Margaret
Barbieri

108

otherwise, it is gibberish. As the dancers and music whip the storm into existence, Peter leans over John's shoulder with an afterthought: "Just a few flashes of lightning. Summer lightning."

Read starts calling different crossfades into his headset the moment the act is over, shading the light levels so the intensity of the storm will alter with the stage manager's cue and the flick of an electrician's finger. Oblivious of the shifting light and occasional darkness, Margaret and Desmond run through the Act 4 *pas de deux*–they're the third cast to have done it this morning. Margaret is costumed fully but not dancing fully. Two fingers of her left hand are taped; she has bent them painfully backward, and Desmond partners her gently.

The girls have an hour to transform themselves for Act 3. Donning her Mazurka boots for the first time, one says "Mazurka chaps, you'd better start lacing your boots now or you're never going to finish. And the laces don't reach–they're not long enough." When "Beginners" is called over the loudspeaker, not one of them is finished dressing.

On stage, Desmond is asking Kim to help him fasten the ornate Rothbart cloak: "This is a hell of a job. It's thousands and thousands of poppers. I'll have to have Velcro. Peter says he doesn't mind about the noise." Carl and Alain march on in lockstep, arms around each other's waists like Tweedledum and

"Tweedledum and Tweedledee": (left to right) Alain Dubreuil and Carl Myers

Tweedledee, with every sequin in eleven trimmings on their Spanish jackets glittering. Both thrones and six of the eight high-backed chairs have been set. Peter shakes his head, laughing, "Philip, you've made my life hell. I've got to find somewhere to *put* all your costumes." Philip smiles back from the stalls like a Cheshire cat and comments mildly that he thinks it looks lovely with them all shoved into corners at the base of the columns.

Placing everyone *and* his costume takes an hour. At 3:30, Peter finally tells Michael Throne, the stage manager, to call "Places" and run the act through at last. Picking up his pre-arranged cue, Stephen Lade swings into the introduction to the Mazurka on the piano and then the entire company swings into Happy Birthday for Peter. He is surprised just leaving the stage for his seat out front, and electrics pins him to the proscenium arch with a follow spot. He stands diffidently in its glare while they sing, swallows hard, and says, "You're a marvellous company. I love you all. Thank you very much."

And with that, they get to work. Siegfried gets a new entrance since too many people and costumes are standing in the way of his old one. David and Galina

Czardas. (left to right) Lynne Wake, David Bintley, Lili Griffiths, Denis Bonner, Nicola Katrak, David Morse

mark to conserve their energy, but everyone else dances as full out as he can. The Czardas girls seem to be moving underwater in their black velvet and gold lamé. "You can't dance in them very well," Lynne Wake admits, "but you feel very glamourous." Watching them from the wings, Grahame sighs, "It's like a Russian fairy tale come true."

The Czardas boys keep dodging their own floor-length sleeves. Serenely still in her lady-in-waiting gown, Dido reaches down her bodice and pulls out an earring. During the Neapolitans, Peter turns to Jeffrey Phillips–oh yes, he's here too now–and whispers, "Isn't there anywhere in Manchester where we can get real tambourines? We must have them."

The vision doesn't appear because the light cue is late. Then the vision girl–someone must be cast, dressed and cued for every performance–trips over the black curtain that hides her behind the vision gauze and nearly falls off her platform. Rothbart's undertatters catch in his robe as he strips off his disguise. And Odile and Rothbart exit up the centre stairs into total darkness, unable to see where they're going.

There is, of course, no time for a second runthrough. Margaret and Desmond, and the second cast Princesses, Czardas, and Spanish boys must all go without their scheduled stage rehearsal. No one is surprised.

Complaints bubble everywhere; whinging dulls their exhaustion and worry. In the canteen, the boys say, "This should be an opera." In the showers, the girls say, "I've never been in such an uncomfortable ballet." In the wardrobe, Jane Cowood says, "It's so hot in here. But it's not bright enough in the other rooms so you can't work anywhere else. The choice is either go blind or sweat to death." Jean Percival is separating Odile's tiara from the frame with the mesh and feathers on it, making the headdress half as large and half as heavy: "This is Galina's. No doubt they'll all want it."

6:00 p.m. onstage. *Shrew* is set for tonight, the piano is in the wings, and they're cuing Hilary by voice while Sherilyn and Carl, with Margaret and Desmond upstage of them, rehearse Black Swan for Christine Anthony's comments. She asks Carl, "What are you thinking during the vision? You mustn't see it. It's like a flash in your mind. She's bewitching you." Then she talks to Sherilyn about phrasing, filling out the music: "You must make everything bigger than you would by your own nature. It's a big stage, big costume." When Sherilyn starts the *manège* of *piqués* and *soutenus*, Christine shouts, "Keep calm. Keep calm. Go on, go on, go on," yelling all through the last twelve counts, the second half of it. "You use up so much strength and energy fighting it. You mustn't fight–just keep going. At least you're getting through it now." "I have trouble getting 'round that upstage left corner. I can't see," Sherilyn protests. "But you *are* getting 'round it," Christine insists.

Wearing her Odile tutu and headdress, Margaret is still refining what the public will see on Saturday as finished and fixed. "Where should I put my foot in this *attitude*?" Desmond adjusts her balance with both hands on her waist as she

111

crooks it behind him, then up over his shoulder, at the back of his head, beside his ear–choosing. He grabs her foot like a telephone receiver and calls, "Hello? Hello?" into the sole of her shoe. "Did you notice," Hilary asks quietly, gathering her music, "that the piano has a swan on it?"

9:00 p.m. Hysteria strikes the *Shrew* cast. Chenca, Carl and most of the corps stand in the wings and giggle helplessly.

26 November. Thursday. 9:00 a.m. The light crew continues focussing. They will stop at 10:30 so class can be held onstage, resume work at 11:45, and continue until 12:30. Christine Anthony wryly describes the class as "a change for them after the foyer. They're all a bit nervy anyway, so one's got to try to keep their spirits up."

9:30 a.m. Gordon is replacing the decorative buckles on the waltz boys' belts with braid. Edward is wearing Siegfried's Act 3 tunic over his checked flannel shirt. Margery Rogers and Jane stayed all night to repair the tutus whose skirts had separated from their bodices in rehearsal. Margery's hands are a blur. "It's no use sewing things together with neat little stitches. You want big strong stitches–they don't show anyway–or they simply come apart. People think it's what's on top, the embroidery, that's important, but it's really what's underneath. The Bolshoi and Kirov do it differently. They stitch right over that bodice closing. The girls have to line up to be stitched in. Really, there's nothing more maddening from a dancer's point of view than to feel whatever you're wearing simply coming apart."

10:20 a.m. A very subdued company gathers for Christine's deliberately encouraging class. Waiting her turn at the side, Sherilyn says, "That six o'clock rehearsal yesterday was the first I've done of Act 3 since the Wells. I was just going to do my solos, with Desmond there, but then Carl showed up so we could do it together. I was going a bit mad never having a chance to do it. Christine is so helpful–I'll miss her. She goes the end of the week."

11:30 a.m. Louise is replacing Rothbart's poppers with Velcro. Philip sits beside her, his face nearly as grey as his sweatshirt after last night's birthday celebration with Peter. But he is awake and alert: "I'm pleased with the way it's coming on. I haven't yet seen it straight through in sequence, so today should be very interesting." And an hour later, he is on stage approving new props. Graham Crew has made two trays to carry the goblets with which Siegfried is toasted in Act 1, and Robin has made cloths to cover the trays. "Am I right," asks Graham, "that the two big tambourines are for the boys and the two smaller ones are for the girls?" "Only Peter Wright would know that," answers Philip. The dancers have punched through the cheap ones, time after time. Robin is blacking the wooden rims of the new ones with magic marker, inside and out, and Philip suddenly remembers that they'll also need ribbons.

When Michael Throne calls "Five minutes," he also announces: "Ladies and gentlemen of the second act, when you hear your call, please come down to the corridor but do NOT come onstage until the scene change is completed." The decision has been made to run Act 1 and 2 with a pause for scene changing but no full interval. The change can't be made with the dancers in the way, but the act can't move ahead quickly enough to stay on schedule if the dancers aren't immediately available once the change is finished.

1:00 p.m. Margaret and Desmond with Alain as Rothbart will dance the dress rehearsal. The orchestra is here for the first time since last Friday. The funeral cortège is complete for the first time ever–dancers, extras, costumes, props, music and lights. No one speaks through the action except Barry Wordsworth. "OK for bassoon?" he calls up to the balcony during the *pas de quatre*. He can only check sound levels and balance while the orchestra is actually playing in the

Barry Wordsworth
and the orchestra

Act 1. Benno's solo in the
pas de quatre: Roland Price

theatre. Peter whispers his notes to Alison; Galina gives hers to Debbie. Philip and Kim huddle together too; in an instant of silence you hear his, "Don't argue with me. Just put it down," and their muffled laughter.

John Seekings, one of two Technical Managers for the Royal Opera House, who keeps an eye on particularly big new productions and all revivals, makes his own list: "Patch and paint P.S. (prompt side) D.S. (downstage) columns. Pin candles to floor. Fix stair carpet firmly. Look at O.P. (opposite prompt) masking. Spray and straighten leaves. Paint tree wires black."

Desmond and Roland Price give full performances in Act 1, and everyone seems more comfortable with the costumes. Between the acts, Kim says, "This company is marvellous about coping, and they know how beautiful they look. If you're trying to whiz around in a heavy costume that's also *hideous*, you're going to be too depressed. But if you're trying to whiz around and you know you look beautiful, half the battle is won."

All goes well with Act 2 until Peter breaks his silence during the *pas de deux*: "Girls, look at your line." The entire stage left line of swans breaks and reforms, straight and ten inches further upstage. When they finish the *pas de deux*, Margaret and Desmond bow, to the empty theatre and each other, acknowledging non-existent applause so that Barry can take the pause into account and gauge his next downbeat accordingly.

Act 3, with the second cast of Princesses. The banners that herald the Queen Mother's arrival have been cut—no time to manoeuvre the cloth or the bodies.

114

White Swan *pas de
deux*. Margaret
Barbieri and
Desmond Kelly

Rothbart's death.
Alain Dubreuil

The first ambassador misses his entrance and everything stops. Benno's circlet goes flying off his head and into the pit. The *pas de six* girls can't hear Barry's crystalline pizzicatto under their latex headdresses. Mazurka men now have wigs and beards. Czardas couples wrinkle their faces at the tempo and grab for each others' hands around the bulk of their costumes to form the wheel. Sami's spangled sleeve catches on the brim of her Spanish hat and is stuck there for sixteen bars. Large black wigs with sequin-dusted buns render the Neapolitan girls unrecognizeable.

Alain has given Rothbart a white mask of make-up with deep hollow eyes. When he enters with Odile after the Black Swan *pas de deux*, Christine Anthony and Marion Tait hiss from the front as if he were a pantomime villain.

Act 4. One swan skids, then falls during the storm.

Desmond tears Rothbart's helmet off during their struggle, and Alain dies a grotesque, silent film death. He calls it his "incredible shrinking man" scene.

Attention splinters as the curtain falls. Barry reminds the orchestra that tonight's call for the "general" dress rehearsal is at 7:00, and that "it's Galina, so it's the other version of the variation in Act 3." Peter discusses lighting cues with Michael Throne: When will the light hit the apotheosis? The funeral cortège? Where is the lightning during the storm? Why can't you see anyone on the centre steps? "They go straight into the dark and come out again into the light. I must have more light on those steps." Then they set the sequence of curtain calls. Then he gives notes to the company, who are scattered about the stalls in dressing gowns and pieces of their costumes:

"Funeral procession must be walking when the curtain goes up." "We had no warning that the curtain was *going* up," Desmond puts in. ". . And a bit tighter together, procession. And the pages must hold their capes to keep them from rustling."

He changes the last three counts of the waltz, and the toast to Siegfried, and asks Anita to clarify one mime gesture. She thanks him; as Robin Snow said, you never stop learning.

"Nikki and Christine, I want you to be like courtesans, highly paid ones, mind you, but tarts for the pleasure of the palace. Not little girls. Don't worry—I've never told you that before. I just changed it." Months after the opening he will tell me that there hadn't been time to work this out as they rehearsed and, although it *had* been his idea all along, he was almost afraid to put it in at the last moment.

"More action for all of you, particularly when Desmond's dancing alone because that's more private.

"The first diagonal of the Polacca is really awful, but we've never really placed that dance onstage, have we? We must do that."

He moves on to Act 3–it makes sense. If he skips Act 2, which is only swans, he can excuse the boys after Act 3 notes. Never keep anyone sitting around is the basic rule; someone else probably needs them if you don't.

"Waltz boys, what's the matter with your double *tours*? One or two of you always falls over.

"How should the Spanish bow? You must work out something. I'll look at it tonight."

Then, "That's all, boys. I do want to tell you I'm full of admiration for you for the way you're coping with everything. You'll find it'll get easier and easier.

"Girls, I must say, in Act 2 and 4 the shoes sound awful. You're all clattering away. If one person has hard shoes, it ruins it for everyone else." Galina says, "They'll be soft by tomorrow night," which gets a rueful laugh of agreement. At this point, the girls feel they'll *never* get off their toes.

"And you've got to be whiter," Peter continues. "I have it from the designer. Any of you have wet-white on today? You must just cake it on."

–"What do we do then? Take it off again for the third act?"

–"Well, it's a short interval. You've only got fifteen minutes."

–"As it is, there's barely time to get up to the loo."

—"Then you'll have to leave it on." The subject of wet-white is closed.

"I think I want to make a change in that diagonal run, because you're all backing up going into the wings. There must be a light and there must be someone to catch you.

"Going down to the floor in Act 4, you're not all together. What count do you go down on?" Madeleine sings the counts and marks the movements; all of them, including Peter, watch and hum and mark with her. "Right. 3 and 4. Are we all agreed?"

One arm of one swan gets a note for crossing in front of the body rather than to the side in the *pas de bourrée*.

7:10 p.m. In the dressing room, Lili Griffiths wails, "Michael wants us on stage and dressed, Philip wants wet-white, Anita wants soft shoes, Peter wants soft shoes. . ." She is ready to cry.

Act 1 waltz. (left to right) Mark Welford, Chenca Williams, Stephen Wicks, Mandy-Jayne Richardson, Nicholas Millington, Jennifer Mills, Mark Francis, Susan Crow

7:15. The general dress rehearsal and a photo call as well for Galina, David and Desmond. Before he raises his baton, Barry turns from the pit and asks the audience, such as it is–friends, wardrobe, and some of the injured–to applaud if they feel like it. Everyone needs it to work out the timing of bows and musical cues.

The waltz girls now have silver bracelets made of leather, two of which come off and must be kicked out of the way. They all gulp for air when they turn upstage; with your back to the audience, you can lick your lips, gasp, grimace, so your smile and calm are firmly in place when you turn back.

Margaret stands in the wings, Polish Princess tutu flaring over her sweat-pants, and directs Odette's Act 2 mime to a brick wall.

The monks escorting the Queen Mother are barefoot. No one has issued them sandals or anything else for their feet.

The Polacca boys, without gloves now, show off the dance and their robes equally, allowing each to complement the other. On the sweeping diagonal exit, they now alternate with the waltz boys as Peter wanted. He called them all to the stage half an hour before curtain to set it.

Electrics has wired and lit two of the four hunting lanterns. With each run-through, another piece of the total picture slips into place.

Act 2 now opens with Rothbart standing centre, not rising out of the leaves as originally planned. Desmond has taken the whiteface make-up even further, covering his entire head with rubber so that, beneath his winged helmet, it looks like a skull.

Benno has disappeared from the start of the *pas de deux* as of this performance, so each half of the swan corps has two more flaps of their wings to use up the extra music.

There is a moment before the end of Act 2 when Odette and the corps revolve, flashing their faces front, then back, like mirrors revolving in tandem. Tonight the synchronization is perfect. You can see in an instant confused identities, black and white, truth and deception. They are beginning to perform.

And they sense it themselves. As she shrugs off her tutu during the break, Sami says, "It feels so much better tonight. There was no atmosphere this afternoon, no feeling–it just felt so dead with no one to play to. Tonight there's real energy. It's completely different. And everyone's starting to get excited."

"These two performances have no relation to each other," adds Dido. "The first time with all the costumes, you've got to see how far you can tilt your head back before your hat falls off. It's different every time."

Act 3. The Neapolitan boys wear new codpieces and belts, and all four tambourines flutter with ribbons. The dance is much slower than they ever rehearsed it, simply because the trumpeter can't play it as fast as a pianist. But it is *still* fast.

Galina has drawn her hair up very high into a topknot and wears the new, lighter, smaller, Odile headdress. She gives an all-out ballerina performance to the nearly empty theatre.

Rothbart's death.
Desmond Kelly

BELOW Black Swan
pas de deux. Galina
Samsova

When Peter tries to make more dancing space by moving the Mazurka couples to the steps upstage right, he discovers Galina there, poised for Odile's solo entrance.

She and David discuss tempo both while they dance and after their variations. It is the last chance they'll have before opening night to get it right.

David finishes his solo with a flourish and, unconsciously, snaps his fingers over his head. The snap rings like a release of tension, a punctuation mark; 'There's *that* prepared,' it says.

Act 4 sails by in minutes, complete with visible lightning, a flash pot, and some thunder during the storm.

It is very late by the time Odette and Siegfried are reunited in a golden glow. The dancers vanish instantly; they will get their notes tomorrow. Peter says he's very pleased and will have some sleep after he has some food. Barry says, "This is the first dress rehearsal of *Swan Lake* in a long time that's been gotten through without a single tantrum." Ron says, "You want one?"

27 November. Friday. Opening night. Although every ticket has been gone for weeks, there is a queue at the box office at 8:45 a.m. And the production is already sold out in Leeds, where it won't appear until February, simply on the strength of its being *Swan Lake*. Christine Anthony gives a slow warm-up barre onstage at 9:45, and at 10:15 Michael Throne switches on the callbox. "Please wear dark rehearsal clothes to this rehearsal if you are not in full costume. Photographs are being taken of the principals, and if you are in dark practice clothes, it will be possible to take you out of the picture." He neither minces words nor spares feelings; business is business, his announcement says. It also says, indirectly, that Louise will be able to whisk most of the costumes out of the dressing rooms and back to production wardrobe so they can be completed and cleaned for tonight.

Only a few people are in costume: Sherilyn, Carl and Alain, Lili Griffiths and Sue Lucas who are the second cast *pas de quatre* girls, and Christine Aitken and Karen Donovan, the second cast Hungarian and Polish Princess respectively. This is their first and only stage call and they are glad to have it, even with the piano in the pit instead of the full orchestra.

Before they begin, Peter gathers them all around him onstage and gives last night's notes.

"Act 3. All the court, much bigger curtseys, right down and up again on the entrance of the ambassadors.

"Big reaction to Rothbart . . . Are you all listening to me? Please do.

"Lili and Denis, you mustn't look straight to the front when you come forward in Czardas. You're giving the audience rather a come-hither look.

"Princesses, the music at the end is very grand. Don't rush your arms.

"Act 4. Sami, I hate to tell you that you get your leg too high, but at one point you do.

"Swans, you must change a count . . . Swans, are you all listening?" Yester-

Black Swan *pas de deux*. Sherilyn Kennedy and Carl Myers. The corps dancers are in dark practice clothes

day's tension has evaporated—everyone is too tired. Nick Ringham listens with his eyes closed: "I'm knackered. It makes a change." The Mazurka boys practice their heel clicks; two of them are on their feet and two are sitting down.

"Would everyone clear? Swans, I want to change an entrance in Act 2, where you get chased on by the boys with the lanterns. I want that whole sequence eight counts later, which means Big Swans will have to come on together."

122

Peter cannot slow down. He resets the swan entrance and changes the Polacca again. His energy runs ahead of the dancers and drags them after it. Finally he says, "We'll cut the procession unless you want to do it for tabs and lights. Yes. Do the procession." Barry cues Hilary, "From the top of page seven," and they begin the last runthrough.

Peter urges the cortège, "Creep. Not a sound with your feet."

The waltz is cut except for the bit the Prince does with the girls, so Carl can practice it. The onstage boys applaud Sue Lucas for her solo in the *pas de quatre*. It's not only that she's danced well, but that the second cast can always use the

Act 4 *pas de deux*.
Sherilyn Kennedy and
Carl Myers

boost to their confidence, and their colleagues know exactly how they feel. Roland, in practice clothes, takes his position for his solo because he hasn't been told not to. At the last moment, Peter calls, "Cut the solo," and he drifts off. Anita murmurs, "Is he relieved!"

Act 2. The swans are working for spacing and silent feet, and marking a lot to save their toes and energy. Alongside Sue and Lili, who are still in their Act 1 make-up, they look bare and pale. Peter tells them to relax during the *pas de deux*, and then to clear completely "for the sake of pictures," but they re-appear on their own at every point where they're supposed to dance, for the sake of Sherilyn and Carl.

Peter gives notes on Acts 1 and 2 during the scene change into Act 3–he doesn't know when he'll have another moment to do it. "Lili and Sue, you must be more courtesan-type ladies. More with the skirt. Polacca boys, when do you lift your arms on the turning limps? On the first four or the second four?" Then

Notes onstage: (left to right) Carl Myers, Sherilyn Kennedy, Peter Wright, Alison Palmer

124

he joins Desmond, Michael Throne and Barry to confer about the vision of Odette in Act 3. Michael must call separate cues for the curtain that reveals her, the light on her, and the lights on stage, and he must set them all on the music rather than the action.

Nobody dances in Act 3 except the principals and the Princesses, but everyone does complete entrances and exits. The Mazurka girls wear their boots to stretch them.

"Vision, you mustn't move 'til the light comes on you." The company also freezes in the dark while the lights change. "Company, move! There must be movement as the light comes on." The cue is still wrong; curtain, swan vision, vision light, stage light, music and company movement are still not coordinated.

The dancers onstage applaud the end of the Black Swan adagio loudly, which Carl accepts with a broad grin and his finger in his mouth. He has just cut it on Sherilyn's bodice.

The second swan vision, after the *pas de deux*, is wrong twice and stops everything twice. The third time it's fine, and there is also smoke on the steps so Rothbart and Odile can make a suitably mysterious exit.

Act 4. "Not too sharp on the *pas de bourrée*," Peter says patiently, and he gets what he wants immediately, from the whole corps, on the repeat of the step.

"Relax. Save your legs." Then "Notes on stage and then we'll do cygnets."

Instead of taking notes, the swans get up and perform all the problem spots again for specific correction. Cygnets rehearse only for tempo; two mark, one dances on full pointe, one on half-pointe.

Sherilyn beams. "I was so relieved after Act 3 that I completely forgot about things in Act 4. I forgot the crying; I forgot lots of things. It was exactly the same with my first *Fille*. I was so relaxed after I got through the 'Fanny Elssler' *pas de deux* that I could barely get through the rest of the ballet."

2:25 p.m. Peter finishes his notes to Carl and Sherilyn, and starts giving them to Galina from last night. The floor around her is thick with pointe shoes. She is testing them for tonight, rising and falling in *relevé* with her head cocked as if listening to the way they feel to her feet. Anita and Debbie say they still have "head and arm" notes from yesterday. "We always have notes there isn't time to give." Clare French mutters, with relief, "There are never notes on a performance, not written-down notes *per se*. If somebody sees something wrong and remembers to tell you, that's a note you'll get, but otherwise not." Peter finishes with Galina and turns next to Michael Throne, complaining that the lightning only struck one side of the stage.

6:00 p.m. The stage door office is crammed with flowers, large bouquets, small posies, overflowing baskets, a red rose for each girl in the corps from the boys' corps. Cards and telegrams overlap on the callboard and spill over onto the bare, surrounding wall. Good wishes and congratulations from the Scenic Studio at the London Opera Centre, from Anita on a card printed, "I proclaim a

Galina Samsova

Anita Landa and
swans

126

royal occasion," from Michael Corder, now in New York. "Sock it to them. Fondest love. Siobhan." "Congratulations on your new production. Mme. Messerer." From Frederick Ashton, from John Tooley, from Norman Morrice and the Royal Ballet Company. "My very best wishes to you all for tonight. You have all worked magnificently and deserve a great success. I thank you from the bottom of my heart. With love, Peter."

In the dressing room. "Does anyone know what time we start on Monday in Birmingham?" is answered by a chorus of "Four o'clock."

Clare: "Just because it's a special night, I can't do my eyebrows."

Mandy: "I'm having the same problem."

Madeleine: "I have to plan everything I'm going to do in that court lady dress ten minutes before I do it. I'm nervous tonight even about tripping over a sleeve or having someone step on your train. Mark Francis almost fell down the stairs tripping over his Mazurka sleeves."

Loudspeaker: "Will all swans please report to Dressing Room Five." Notes for Act 4, they all groan, but instead it's Ron, who grins and says "I've come to wish you luck," and produces a giant box of chocolates from behind his back.

Clare: "Oh. Wet-white. That's what I was supposed to be doing."

Janis: "Is anyone else scared?" She puts her hand on her stomach and stares blankly at her own reflection.

6:15 p.m. In running wardrobe, Brian is still at the machine, sewing elastic to the men's tights. Henry is restyling Act 1 boys' wigs. "From the dress rehearsal, with all the extras getting to wear them, it makes it a bit messy." David Bintley is sitting in the canteen, fully clothed; he's not on until Czardas in Act 3. "Actually, I'm shaking. I'm nervous for everyone who's got bits to do before that."

Warming up onstage: (left to right) Sherilyn Kennedy, Nicholas Millington, Galina Samsova

THE PALACE THEATRE MANCHESTER

Friday 27th November 1981

Sadler's Wells Royal Ballet

First performance of a new production

Swan Lake

Odette-Odile	*Galina Samsova*
Prince Siegfried	*David Ashmole*
The Queen Mother	*Anita Landa*
Baron von Rothbart	*Desmond Kelly*
Benno, Prince Siegfried's friend	*Roland Price*

ACT I

Prince's companions — *Susan Crow, Jennifer Mills, Mandy-Jayne Richardson, Chenca Williams, Mark Francis, Nicholas Millington, Mark Welford, Stephen Wicks*

Two Courtesans — *Christine Aitken, Nicola Katrak*

Court ladies, courtiers, ladies in waiting — *Artists of Sadler's Wells Royal Ballet*

PAUSE
of approximately 4 minutes

ACT II

Cygnets — *Ann Carol, Lili Griffiths, Sandra Madgwick, Petal Miller,*

Two Swans — *June Highwood, Mandy-Jayne Richardson*

Swans — *Artists of Sadler's Wells Royal Ballet*

INTERVAL
of approximately 15 minutes

ACT III

Master of Ceremonies — *Ronald Plaisted*

Pas de six — *Susan Lucas, Roland Price, Susan Crow, Bess Dales, Michael O'Hare, Iain Webb*

Hungarian Princess — *Sherilyn Kennedy*

Polish Princess — *Margaret Barbieri*

Italian Princess — *Petal Miller*

Czardas — *Nicola Katrak, David Morse, Karen Donovan, Lili Griffiths, David Bintley, Denis Bonner*

Mazurka — *Clare French, Franziska Merky, Jennifer Mills, Mandy-Jayne Richardson, Mark Francis, Nicholas Millington, Derek Purnell, Stephen Wicks*

Neapolitan Dance — *Ann Carol, Sandra Madgwick, Grahame Lustig, Nicholas Ringham*

Spanish Dance — *June Highwood, Samira Saidi, Alain Dubreuil, Carl Myers*

Ambassadors, pages, guards, attendants, courtiers — *Artists of Sadler's Wells Royal Ballet*

INTERVAL
of approximately 15 minutes

ACT IV

Swans, cygnets — *Artists of Sadler's Wells Royal Ballet*

Conductor: Barry Wordsworth

The performance will end at approximately 10.25 p.m.

Subject to alteration

The boys' dressing room is very quiet indeed.

David Ashmole and Mark Francis are warming up onstage, gripping the moulding on the columns for a barre. Neither sees the other; both are wholly self-absorbed, private, screwing down their nerves and concentration.

7:00 p.m. Peter is standing at the lift in black tie, with Michael Soffe, also in black tie, discussing light cues at the end of Act 1 with two electricians in blue jeans. Philip joins them, looking right at home in the black and white of his evening dress, and says to Peter, "It is well we don't have to go on tonight. We couldn't stand up."

At fifteen minutes, Galina is warming up holding onto the upstage column. She wears plastic pants, leotard, full make-up and her Odette headdress. The "duvets" for the court officials lie in three heaps on the stage, waiting like pets for their dancers.

At the "Five minutes" call—which is at 7:20 since the calls are always five minutes ahead of the actual clock time—Michael Throne reminds everyone wearing large costumes which the wardrobe has to arrange on them to be down on stage in plenty of time for the "Beginners" call at 7:25. By now, he needn't remind them that there is only the one lift and that it is not wide enough for more than one hoopskirt at a time.

Stephen Wicks escorts Marion on stage to wish everyone luck; she is wearing silver-grey silk with fringe, a flapper feather in her hair, and silver sandals. Alison is in red Indian cotton, Britt, the physiotherapist, in a gold lamé jumpsuit, Debbie in maroon velvet. The theatre is packed, buzzing with anticipation, standees at every level. "Stand by, please," Michael Throne calls politely, and Barry heads for the pit. He is probably the only man in the theatre who is completely comfortable in evening dress, since he wears it for every evening performance. No one makes a speech.

The cortège passes so smoothly, so silently, that it seems like a dream or a subliminal image that registers without our actually seeing it.

Act 1. The waltzing couples play to the Prince. The court ladies glide about graciously and chat. Mandy's bracelet comes off. There is applause in the stalls two notes before the end of the waltz.

The second nun falls coming on, just at the corner of the up left column. The monks help her up and escort her off. No one sees.

The *pas de quatre* is nervous; even Roland, whose technique rarely falters, misses his first double *tour en l'air*. Nikki forgets a step while walking with the Prince. Roland misses the last *pirouette* in his solo, turning at an angle and with a wobble. And no one knows, no one sees. They see beautiful dancing. There are bravos as they finish, and applause too for the Polacca boys as they disappear into the gathering darkness of the enchanted evening.

Act 2. The swans calculate their spacing as they come on. Lines are straight, *piquées arabesques* held, but nerves ruffle the smooth edges of their ensemble dance. Even Galina is nervous, slightly cool and withdrawn in the *pas de deux*, a

White Swan *pas de deux*. Galina Samsov and David Ashmole

Act 3 *pas de six*. (left to right) Susan Crov Michael O'Hare, Susan Lucas, Rolanc Price, Bess Dales, Ia Webb

130

bar early with the last phrase of her solo. But from the front, Odette trembles only with fear of Rothbart and the depth of her feeling for Siegfried.

Overheard in the circle bar at the first interval: "You don't like it? I *love* it."

Act 3. The *pas de six* boys spiral into their jumps, exploding like silent fireworks, and earn themselves a sharp burst of applause before the girls join them. There is applause too after the Princesses and a sprinkling of it, like a whisper of delight, at the mere sight of the spectacular Czardas couples.

Mazurka. The girls point their booted feet. The wheel fits like clockwork; hands meet and mesh like polished gears. With an inspired flourish of gallantry, Stephen Wicks kisses Franziska's hem after their brisk solo turn around the floor.

Neapolitan. The trumpeter plays as fast as a pianist, and excitement makes the dancers rush as well. If they moved any faster, gravity couldn't contain them and they'd be whirling into space like shooting stars. Grahame falls, but is up in the same movement. Applause drowns the last sharp slap on the tambourines.

Odile's topskirt, hot from Margery Rogers' hands, is newly bejeweled with blue and silver, like streaks of water, that glisten all the way to the gods. And

Neapolitan Dance
(left to right) Nicholas
[...]ingham, Ann Carol,
[...]rahame Lustig,
[...]andra Madgwick

131

Black Swan *pas de deux*. Galina Samsov and David Ashmole with vision

when Galina stops dead in a flat-out backbend in David's hands at the start of the *pas de deux*, there isn't a sound anywhere in the theatre, in the world.

David doesn't simply rise to the opening night; he soars beyond it. His solo flies, higher and more joyous than ever, lifting the audience with it. Galina flashes through hers, glittering with Odile's malice, and holds the pose at the end, knowing the audience is hers and their attention is pinned to her immobility. Her smile only surfaces with her bow, as if Odile is too haughty, too clever to smile. Nervous perhaps or tired, she then falters on her last *fouettés*, running out of strength or breath before the music runs out. David places himself stage centre, pushes off, and does six *pirouettes* on the beats to fill the time and space she has left empty. He uses them as preparation for his own *grands pirouettes* as if he'd planned it all along.

The second vision works perfectly. As does the mime, the Velcro, the smoke on the steps, and the entire end of the act.

Overheard in the stalls bar at the second interval: "I say! The black one looks just like the white one." Philip and Peter slip through the pass door from the front of the house to the stage. "I hope Galina hasn't hurt herself." Philip's words are almost lost in the delighted chatter of the audience. As is Peter's low answer, "I'm sure she has."

"Does it look very nervous out there?" Anita asks quietly. "Everyone's so jittery."

Act 4. The swans watch each other out of the corners of their wide, clear eyes, space themselves perfectly, and dance as if they've never needed a note. The wedge glides forward silently, the arms fold forward ("1 and 2, 2 and 3") and open back again as if hinged together.

Everywhere the girls have sat is wet. Galina slips during the *pas de deux* but doesn't fall, and the slip seems Odette's premonition of doom, so powerful is the sad lyricism of the duet of parting.

They take seven full stage calls—"that's four extra," says Michael Soffe—and apparently endless bows before the curtain. In the gods, people stomp and cheer. In the more decorous stalls, they cheer quite contentedly without stomping. Flowers flood the stage, lapping at Galina's feet, dappling the swans with brilliance as the boys' roses are formally presented, one to each of them, and the

Act 4 *pas de deux*.
Galina Samsova and
David Ashmole

133

Act 4. The wedge of swans: "Arms fold forward . . . and open back again as if hinged together."

Opening night curtain call. (front row, left to right) Lili Griffiths, June Highwood, Roland Price, Barry Wordsworth, Philip Prowse, David Ashmole (partially hidden), Galina Samsova, Peter Wright, Desmond Kelly, Mandy-Jayne Richardson, Petal Miller

boys watch from the wings in their street clothes. Peter and Philip bow to the audience, to each other, to Galina, to the assembled applauding company, and the curtain falls at last and stays down.

Triumph and fatigue bloom in Galina's face as Sir John Tooley and Peter flank her, like an honour guard arranged in a proud tableau. Wrapped in her pink silk dressing gown, Anita stands in the wings with Bess Dales, who is still in her swan tutu, clutching her rose. Bess bends her head to catch Anita's words through the laughter swirling around them and asks a question. Anita is already giving notes.

★   ★   ★

If this were a film, the story would end there, with that flushed, exultant scene of success. Or with Peter, poking his grinning face around the door of the corps dressing room twenty minutes later to say, "Thank you very much. You were really wonderful, the fourth act especially. But the second act was the best you've ever done it." But opening night of *Swan Lake* is only Friday night, and an audience . . . no, two audiences have already booked their seats for Saturday. Was the first performance the end of a long, arduous process, or only the beginning of one?

"It's going to be a hard day for them," Anita sighs sympathetically, as they slip by the callboard Saturday morning without giving it a glance and trudge upstairs to change for class. Dido echoes her in the dressing room: "It's going to be hard to do it after that excitement last night–do it well and go on doing it well." Lili Griffiths is even more blunt: "Now we can get over being scared and start settling into it." More practical matters press on them this morning than parties, flowers and opening night chocolates: "I'll have to leave class early to clean my shoes." "It's Christine's last day. It's a tragedy. What will we do in Birmingham next week when we really need her?"

Everyone without exception comes to her last class: Sherilyn and Carl who will dance the matinée, Desmond and Margaret who dance tonight, David and

Act 2. Sherilyn Kennedy

136

t 2. Carl Myers

Galina, all here. Mandy is wearing a new turquoise leotard. "Actually, it's Sue Crow's. We wear each other's to keep from getting bored. I thought I'd put it on for 'the morning after.'" They are all quite ready to return to normal, and begin their *pliés* with gratitude for their familiarity.

Not half an hour later, Mandy is back in the dressing room, stripping off her wet leotard and stepping slowly into a hot shower: "I've hurt my groin. Well, I did it a long time ago, but it hasn't been too bad recently. But it was cold on stage during class and I was stiff from being so tense last night, and I finally wrenched it. I'll just dance with Deep Heat on it." Anita comes looking for her: "I saw her limp off. Is she all right? It doesn't sound too bad, and she's determined to dance on it. That's the main thing." She wouldn't be so worried if opening night had been closing night too; there would be no matinée, no travelling, no Birmingham next week. But the production cannot bear an injury any better now than it could two days ago. Life may have been all champagne and cheers last night, but today it's business as usual. The show, and the tour, must go on.

And, of course, they do. At the matinée, Mandy's injury is invisible; she simply smiles and dances. Carl's haunted face sends a shiver through the audience as he senses Rothbart's ominous presence at the opening of Act 2. Sherilyn completes the *manège* in Act 3 with apparent ease, and completes the thirty-two *fouettés* as well. She is then so relieved that she becomes spontaneous, throwing her head back with a chilling soundless laugh as Siegfried finally betrays Odette. After the curtain falls, Anita hugs her and tells her "it was a star performance."

Act 3. Sherilyn Kennedy

RIGHT Petal Miller as
the Neapolitan
Princess

FAR RIGHT Karen
Donovan as the Polish
Princess

Act 1 *pas de quatre:*
(left to right) Susan
Lucas, Carl Myers,
Lili Griffiths

Act 2. Margaret
Barbieri and
Desmond Kelly

Black Swan *pas de
deux*. Margaret
Barbieri and
Desmond Kelly

RIGHT Act 4: Swans in a mist of dry ice

BELOW Act 4 *pas de deux*. Marion Tait and Alain Dubreuil

Peter Wright
rehearsing Sherilyn
Kennedy

At the five minute call that evening, a rested and refreshed Galina twirls gaily in a blue silk dress and says, with a flickering smile, "I spend so much time in black and white that it's nice to be able to relax." She will be a spectator tonight instead of a swan. Sitting back comfortably, she will see Margaret, Desmond and Alain lead the company to another ovation. Will all the choices and changes and counts of the last several months line up in her mind's eye as the dancers sweep confidently through the three hours? Or will she let the magical illusion bewitch her, as it bewitches the audience?

In Act 4, there is much more mist from the dry ice than ever before, and the swans seem to billow out of it in their tutus. "I couldn't believe it," Dido crows as she leaves the theatre. "When it dispersed, I was on my mark."

That was only a day after opening night. Within a week, the reviews are piling up. Heaping praise on Peter, Galina and Philip in equal measure, they call their *Swan Lake* "an unqualified triumph," "splendid," "sensationally sumptuous," "thoughtful and dramatic," and "not only an immediate success, but a fine investment for the future."

A month later—on December 31 to be precise—in Monte Carlo, Marion Tait finally dances her first Odette-Odile, partnered by Alain Dubreuil.

And nearly a month after that, on January 26, 1982, the 1981 Standard Award for the Most Outstanding Achievement in Ballet is presented to Peter Wright for his direction of the Sadler's Wells Royal Ballet in general and his production of *Swan Lake* in particular. Only weeks earlier, he had said to me, "I never did *Swan Lake* before because I never had the opportunity, but I always wanted to, as I think everyone does. John (Cranko), Kenneth (MacMillan), Fred (Ashton), Balanchine . . . we all have ideas about things and we want to see them realized. I really decided to do it while I was working with John in Stuttgart. I was his associate producer and ballet master. He did the ballet very quickly and left quite a bit to me, and I thought I'd love to be doing my own. I've been battling to do it here for seven years.

"The classics are a necessity, absolutely essential, for a company like this, because of the corps work. *Beauty* is incredibly difficult to do on tour because of the numbers—you have to have the whole spectacle. But I could do *Swan Lake* and be satisfied with it with even fewer people than we've got. It's not so hard to make a good production. To make a *special* production is hard."

And of course he does not even speculate as to whether his production will be special. But perhaps that is logical too.

"The thing about the creative process," says Philip, "is that you must hide it. You're tempting fate if you don't. You must say, 'Oh well, we'll slap a bit of paint on that,' because if you say, 'This is going to be important, great art,' God will be listening and he'll say, '*And* you'll get it wrong.'"